Wild Fish & Game
COOKBOOK

RECIPES, STORIES & ILLUSTRATIONS BY
JOHN MANIKOWSKI

PHOTOGRAPHS BY
ZEVA OELBAUM

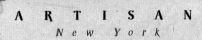

ARTISAN
New York

Production director: Hope Koturo
Food stylists: Catherine Chatham
                Susan Ehlich

Published in 1997 by Artisan,
a division of Workman Publishing Company, Inc.
708 Broadway, New York, NY 10003-9555

Library of Congress Cataloging-in-Publication Data
Manikowski, John.
        Wild fish & game cookbook / recipes, stories & illustrations by
John Manikowski ; photographs by Zeva Oelbaum.
        Includes index.
        ISBN 1-885186-50-X
        1. Cookery (Game) 2. Cookery (Fish) 3. Cookery (Wild Foods)
I. Title.
TX751.M33 1997
641.6'9—dc21

                                    97-16187

Printed in Italy

10   9   8   7   6   5   4   3   2   1

FIRST PRINTING

Dedication

This book is dedicated to Dad,

who never did teach me to

fish and hunt but that's all right—

he taught me other things:

to work with my hands, to love

gardening, to appreciate music

and, unknowingly, to have patience.

Contents

Introduction 8

Soups, Terrines, Pâtés
& Other Appetizers
11

Trout, Shad, Walleye, Northern Pike
& Other Fish
38

Ducks, Pheasants, Quail, Grouse
& Other Game Birds
66

Venison, Elk, Caribou, Wild Boar
& Other Furred Game
102

Vegetable Accompaniments
161

Desserts
171

Cooking Notes & Basic Recipes 179

Acknowledgments 184

Conversions 185

Mail-Order Sources 186

Index 188

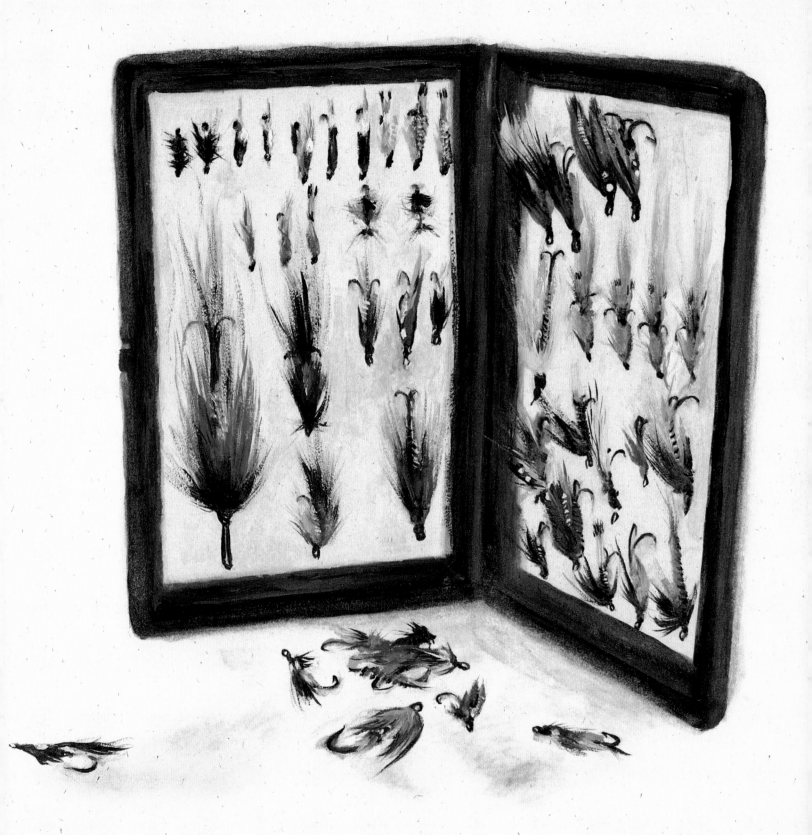

Introduction

It tastes like chicken." Well maybe some of it does, but in general, no, most wild game does not taste like chicken. Why not? Another saying is considerably more appropriate: "You are what you eat." It stands to reason that the flavorful juniper berries savored by ruffed grouse ultimately give the grouse its flavor, unobtainable from any other bush.

A mallard's diet, like that of many ducks, is diverse, creating a rich flavor. But a diving duck, such as a merganser, eats primarily fish, snails, and clams and has an unpleasant, fishy taste.

Picture a flock of mallards in the wetland where they were hatched. At first, they feed on aquatic invertebrates, insects, and crustaceans. By late July the duck's feeding habits begin to change. They eat primarily vegetation, laying down much needed fat for the upcoming migration to warmer climates.

Days are becoming shorter and temperatures fall, triggering the stimulus to migrate. They stop briefly in Michigan's Upper Peninsula, eating a generous supply of corn and barley. After resuming their flight southward, one duck is brought down by the keen eyesight of a hunter (a local fishing guide, actually). But a good number of ducks manage to avoid hunters' shots during the long migration to their winter grounds in Louisiana. By late December, the ducks have adapted to their southern cuisine—fewer aquatic insects and invertebrates and a lot of cultivated rice.

One day during the Louisiana hunting season, a hunter jumps up from his blind in a bayou and claims a greenhead. A few days later, the southern hunter makes a call to a guide he knows from fishing trips to the Upper Peninsula. They chat a bit, he books a fishing trip, and they exchange recipes for the duck they had each recently prepared (they pride themselves on being fine cooks).

You realize, I'm sure, that each of these two ducks will have a different flavor and perhaps texture, even though both were reared in the same breeding grounds, possibly hatched from the same nest. The Louisiana duck will have flown hundreds of miles, working off much of the accumulated fat, and will have changed its feeding habits. Of course, it's difficult to compare unless tasted side-by-side, but most hunters are keenly aware of the acquired, wild taste, which is one of the primary reasons hunters hunt.

Venison, too, can vary in taste. Deer eat apples, flowers, and winter buds and berries in one region, while in another place and season they eat leaves, ants, soybeans, and legumes. Most hunters, of course, find a poorly field-dressed piece of venison repugnant, or a grilled steak from a buck shot during the rut musty, dry, and strong. On the other hand, what hunter does not enjoy the tender backstrap of a rabbit baked in mustard, red wine, and fresh herbs? Who cannot conjure up a midwestern cornfield while carving a South Dakota pheasant, or remember the flush of flapping wings while pan-frying several livery woodcock for hungry hunter-friends? The rewards of the hunter are many—honestly earned and highly prized. We love that hint of the outdoors that has sprinkled its magic seasoning over our pots, plates, and palates.

The world has been feasting on wild fish and game for millennia. Bas reliefs dating to Mesopotamian times and

Egyptian tomb paintings depict the hunting of animals. Even the Bible states: "There are beasts ye shall eat . . . the hart, the roebuck and the fallow deer . . ."

Hunters far and wide, from the Everglades of Florida, to the fields of Alabama, across the plains of North Dakota, still comb the water and land where the Choctaw, Cherokee, and Sioux fished and hunted. Many of our present-day cooking techniques are based on Native American cuisine. Before refrigeration, smoking was a frequent preservative. How convenient to simply grab a hunk of buffalo jerky while on horseback, traversing the midwestern prairie. Smoked fish could be kept far longer than fresh fish. Sun-dried berries were often pounded into pemmican or added to soups and stews for variety of taste and the vitamins they contained.

We are grateful to the Chippewa for wild rice; the Natchez gave us fried corn fritters; the Sioux, cornmeal cakes. The Pueblos made spicy tortilla soup, the Northwest coast's Gitksans planked salmon on a piece of cedar sprinkled with juniper berries and propped up next to glowing hot coals. Bob Black Bull—a member of Montana's Blackfeet Nation who lives north of Browning—still makes a mean loaf of Bannock bread, imbedded with freshly picked serviceberries (page 130). We have learned much from these preparations.

What about farm-raised game? A contemporary farmer has learned to feed his herd of fallow deer choice grains like wheat, alfalfa, and corn. One of the tastiest venison chops I've eaten was supplied to Charleston Restaurant in Hudson, New York, by Highland Farms in the Hudson River Valley. Some customers wince at the thought of being served "Bambi," but a good introduction to wild game can now be had in restaurants throughout the country.

But what *about* farm-raised game? Well, wouldn't you rather eat pheasant, duck, turkey, deer, or buffalo that has spent its life running around outdoors, free of hormone injections, antibiotics, steroids, vitamins, and other chemicals? I would. There is a modest, but increasing, number of entrepreneurial growers who today feed the public healthier foods than existed even a decade ago.

Let's look at some facts: the fat content of beef is 25.1% (per 100 grams of cooked meat). Buffalo yields only 2.8% grams of fat, venison—a mere 5%. Both buffalo and venison are low in cholesterol and high in protein, potassium, and iron. Buffalo has only 50 calories per ounce; venison, 46.3 calories per ounce. (One egg contains 75 calories.) Wild pheasant has 38% less fat than domestic turkey. In general, wild game meat is an exceptionally good source of protein, iron, and also vitamin B-12, available only in animal products.

Fish are high in protein too, but are also rich in phosphorous, magnesium, copper, iron, iodine, cobalt, zinc, fluoride and the B vitamins. Even the fattiest of fish, the eel, has less fat than beef. Most fish are low in fat, ranging from the leanest, such as cod, sole, perch and bass (1-4%), to oily fish, such as salmon (8-12%) and tuna, one of the oiliest, (12-13%). However, the fat in seafood is polyunsaturated fat, so-called "good fat." (*Saturated* fat is the artery-clogging type; bad fat.) Calcium is supplied by eating anchovies and canned sardines, tuna, or salmon—the extra bit of calcium coming from bones that soften enough during the canning process to be easily digested.

So wild fish and game come to the table leaner and healthier than beef, chicken, pork, and lamb. The all-around sportsman, the one who fishes and hunts, benefits the most because of the game he has frozen, smoked, cured, dried, canned, pickled or otherwise put up for the larder.

Aside from the natural health benefits of wild fish and game, the recipes in this book, for the most part, contain only small quantities of cream, butter (even though I find it hard to cook for myself without it), milk, eggs, salt and pre-salted products and ingredients considered rich and unhealthy. There are other ways to influence otherwise bland-tasting foods; herbs, spices, rich stocks, smoking, fruits, and nuts in various combinations makes food taste good.

But the work involved in producing good food takes time, time, time. Anyone who enjoys being in the kitchen knows that. It takes perseverance, drive, inner as well as physical strength, endurance, focus, organization, and talent to tend to a first-rate kitchen. Chefs and cooks around the world know the complexities of a startling, wonderful dish. Sometimes it can only be reproduced, never recorded.

One day, I decided to cook barbecued ribs at home. They were called the "best ever" by a native North Carolinian savvy to ribs, a compliment I still cherish. Why were they superior? Because I took a tremendous amount of time to prepare them. First I made a bath of beer, water, some Worcestershire sauce, a little tomato sauce, and some frozen veal stock. After simmering the ribs for about an hour, I removed them, transferred them to my portable backyard smoker, and left them to smoke slowly for about 2½ hours. I then brushed them with barbecue sauce and put them under the broiler for about 15 minutes until they were heated and the sauce slightly charred.

Nearly four hours to produce delicious ribs? It may appear to be an inordinate amount of time, but it wasn't. The results: deliciously smoky, woodsy-flavored ribs; enjoyed, disproportionately, in a few short minutes (I think good meals should be spread out over time and be slowly savored, along with a good bottle of wine). I didn't write down that particular recipe but I wonder if anyone would go to the trouble to make ribs like that at home, for themselves. Some would. (Barbecued Mountain Sheep Ribs on page 149 come close, however, and the recipe can be adapted for any ribs.)

I may stretch some readers' tolerance, I think, with the Cassoulet and the Duck Confit recipes and perhaps a handful of others, but I make no apologies. Just roll up your sleeves, turn on some good music, fire up the stove, uncork a good bottle of wine, and allow everything its proper time to marinate, breathe, and cook. And then savor it all slowly, with enjoyment. If you're deeply moved, toss some cornmeal to the four winds, whisper a prayer of thanks to the spirit gods, and perform a traditional dance out of respect for the animal who has graciously bestowed its life-giving powers upon you. Or just sit down and enjoy wild game.

Soups, Terrines, Pâtés

& Other Appetizers

French Canadian Pea Soup

Serves 6 to 8

1 quart unsalted veal or beef stock

2 12-ounce bottles beer

1 pound dried yellow peas

1-2 large smoked ham hocks, about 1½ pounds

1 medium onion, chopped (about 1 cup)

8 garlic cloves, diced

2 carrots, peeled and cut into chunks

2 stalks celery, cut into chunks

1 apple, peeled, cored, and cut into chunks

1 tablespoon canola or vegetable oil

½ pound smoked game sausage or sweet Italian sausage

2 tablespoons butter

8 juniper berries, crushed

4 small dried chipotle peppers

1½ teaspoons mustard seeds

1 tablespoon ground coriander

½ teaspoon cracked black peppercorns

Julienned carrots, for garnish

THE FIRST TIME I made French Canadian pea soup was over a fire beside a stunningly beautiful Canadian stream. Naturally, I have rarely been able to duplicate the flavor, perhaps because of the one important ingredient that is usually missing—the bracing Canadian air.

The crisply sautéed sausage in this recipe adds another dimension to a filling soup that might easily serve as a main course.

Combine the stock, beer, peas, ham hock, ½ cup onion, and ¾ of the garlic in a stockpot over high heat. Add 3 quarts of water and bring to a boil, then turn down the heat to medium-low, cover, and simmer for 1 hour.

Combine the carrots, celery, remaining onion, apple, and remaining garlic in the bowl of a food processor. Pulse 6-8 times, but do not puree. Remove 3 cups of this mixture from the processor and set aside. (Any remaining mixture may be frozen for another use.)

Heat the oil in a large skillet over medium-high heat. (If your game sausage is low in fat, you may need to use more oil.) Crumble the sausage into small bits and fry until very crispy and dark brown, but not burnt. Drain, reserving the oil, and set aside the sausage. Return about 1 tablespoon of the oil and add the butter to the pan. Turn the heat to medium-low, add the vegetable mixture and sausage, and sauté for 8-10 minutes, until the vegetables are soft, stirring occasionally.

After the peas have cooked for 1 hour, add the vegetable-sausage mixture, the juniper berries, chipotle peppers, mustard seed, coriander, and peppercorns. Continue simmering, covered, for 2-2½ hours, until the peas have completely broken down. Remove the meat from the ham hock, dice, and return to the pot. Discard the bone and fat. Remove the chipotle peppers.

Ladle the soup into large warmed bowls and serve immediately, garnished with julienned carrots.

Jerusalem Artichoke Soup

DON'T PLANT JERUSALEM ARTICHOKES unless: (1) you love them and plan to eat this cousin of the sunflower for the rest of your life, and (2) you have abundant space outside of your garden.

These "sunchokes," as they are also called, multiply more rapidly and nearly as widely—although underground—as a patch of squash. They are unstoppable but delicious, with an unusual nutlike flavor and texture.

Native Americans made Jerusalem artichokes into soups and also ate them raw. You can slice them thin and add to salads or sauté briefly with string beans and fresh tarragon as a crunchy vegetable side dish.

2 pounds Jerusalem artichokes

2 tablespoons butter

1 medium onion, diced (about 1 cup)

6 cups unsalted veal or chicken stock

1 large potato, peeled and diced

2 tablespoons chopped chives or scallions

1 tablespoon stemmed fresh thyme

½ teaspoon salt

1 teaspoon freshly ground black pepper

Julienned Jerusalem artichokes and chopped parsley, for garnish

Scrub the Jerusalem artichokes (no need to peel them) with a stiff brush and divide into two equal piles. Thinly slice one half and set aside. Roughly chop the remaining half.

Bring 3 quarts of water to a boil in a medium saucepan and add the chopped artichokes. Cover, bring to a boil, and cook for 10-15 minutes, until soft. Drain and transfer the cooked chokes to the bowl of a food processor and puree for about 30 seconds (or mash with a potato masher) until smooth. Set aside.

Melt the butter in a large saucepan and sauté the onion for about 5 minutes, until translucent. Add the stock, potato, chives, thyme, salt, pepper, and all the artichokes. Simmer for about 20 minutes, until the potatoes are thoroughly cooked.

Ladle into soup bowls and serve immediately, garnished with a few slices of julienned raw artichokes and chopped parsley.

Callaloo Soup with Cornmeal Dumplings

Serves 4

2 tablespoons butter

½ teaspoon canola or vegetable oil

1 large red onion, finely chopped (about 1½ cups)

2 garlic cloves, finely chopped

½ pound venison sausage, crumbled

½ pound okra, finely chopped

3 scallions, sliced, with some of the greens

¼ cup dry white wine

¾ pound chopped spinach (about 6 cups)

¼ pound chopped arugula (about 2 cups)

1 can sweetened coconut cream

4 cups unsalted chicken stock

2 tablespoons chopped fresh thyme

2 tablespoons chopped fresh tarragon

2 tablespoons cracked black peppercorns

½ teaspoon salt

¾ pound crabmeat (optional)

Cornmeal dumplings (see recipe following)

AFTER TRAVELING THROUGH the Caribbean and stopping at thirteen different islands, I couldn't help but try a soup recurring on many restaurant menus. Callaloo is associated with the Caribbean because of its primary ingredient, dasheen (or taro leaves), which grow on a bush with edible roots. Spinach makes a suitable substitute. Two other primary ingredients are okra and coconut milk.

The dish varies from island to island; it often includes crab claws or crabmeat, and pork or bacon to deepen the taste. My version includes some of these ingredients and yields a rich broth.

Callaloo soup is often served with dumplings, which makes it a satisfying main course.

Melt the butter with the oil in a large skillet over medium heat. Add the onion, garlic, and sausage and sauté until the sausage is crispy. Drain off all but about 1 tablespoon of the oil and add the okra and scallions. Simmer for 4-5 minutes, until the okra is soft. Add the wine and reduce by one-third, about 4 minutes. Add the spinach and arugula and stir until wilted, about 2 minutes. Add the coconut cream, chicken stock, thyme, tarragon, peppercorns, and salt. Cover and cook over medium heat for about 30 minutes, until the vegetables are integrated with the liquid. Add the crabmeat during the last 5 minutes of cooking. Ladle into soup bowls and place 1-2 dumplings in each bowl. Serve warm.

Cornmeal Dumplings

Heat the butter in large saucepan over medium heat and add the onion. Sauté for 6-8 minutes, until translucent. Add the milk, thyme, pepper, and salt. Bring to a boil, then immediately lower the heat and slowly add the cornmeal, whisking constantly, until the mixture becomes smooth. Turn off the heat and remove the cornmeal from the pot with a rubber spatula. Refrigerate for at least 2 hours. (The mixture will keep for about 2 days, but is best when used fresh.)

When completely chilled, use an ice-cream scoop to make smoothly rounded balls. (One per person will do if you use a large scoop, two if a small one.)

In a large pot, heat about a quart of vegetable oil to 350°F and gently lower the cornmeal balls into the oil to cook for about 10 minutes, until lightly browned.

Serve warm in Callaloo Soup.

VARIATION: If you don't want to fry the dumplings, you can simmer them in boiling water for 10-15 minutes, until firm.

1 tablespoon butter

1 small white onion, finely chopped (about ½ cup)

¾ cup whole milk

1 tablespoon chopped fresh thyme

1 tablespoon cracked black peppercorns

1 teaspoon salt

1 cup yellow cornmeal

Vegetable oil, for frying

Home-Smoked Salmon

1 salmon fillet, about 2½-3 pounds

1 quart curing solution (see page 183)

½ cup homemade mayonnaise

½ cup Dijon mustard

¼ cup chopped dill

Recommended Wine

Serve with Champagne: Ruinart, Champagne R de Ruinart Brut NV, is a great bubbly wine that has fruit as well as coffee, vanilla, and mushroom flavors. It is well balanced and smooth, ideally paired with Home-Smoked Salmon.

SALMON IS A NATURALLY oily fish and lends itself to this hot-smoking technique (cold smoking requires an elaborate contraption and far more time). You may smoke any species of salmon. I prefer King (Chinook) from the West Coast, but have more often used the unrelated Atlantic salmon. You can use trout in this recipe if you wish.

The fillet needs to cure overnight, refrigerated, before you smoke it. This salmon is best served warm from the smoker as an appetizer or a main course. Home-smoked salmon is best served warm, but it will keep in the refrigerator for up to 6 days.

Lay the salmon fillet in a large glass or ceramic container (you may have to cut the fillet in half to fit) and pour the curing solution over it. Cover and refrigerate overnight.

The next day, light a charcoal fire in a backyard smoker. (See page 180.)

When the charcoal is gray and hot, remove the salmon from the cure (discarding the curing solution), pat dry, and place, skin side down, on an oiled wire rack over the wood chips. Cover and smoke for 2-2½ hours, until the internal temperature of the fish is 140-145°F. Maintain the internal temperature of the smoker at 250-300°F. Replenish the charcoal and wood chips as needed.

Mix the mayonnaise, mustard, and dill. Serve with the warm salmon.

Marinated Smelt

MY FATHER LOVED FRESH SMELT. He would buy more than we could eat from fishermen returning from Lake Superior after the rainbow smelt run. I learned how to freeze fish from him. He would simply immerse as many of the little sardinelike, headless fish in a clean half-gallon cardboard milk container and then fill it with water. Frozen in this manner, the fish do not come into contact with air, the culprit of freezer burn. Many foods may be frozen in this manner and will last longer than those merely wrapped in plastic wrap or foil.

Heat the oil in a large, heavy skillet over medium heat. Place the smelt and flour in a paper bag, shake, and remove fish, brushing off excess flour. Add the smelt and sauté for 3-4 minutes, until lightly browned, then turn and cook 2-3 minutes more, until golden brown. Remove from the pan and drain on paper towels. Cover and refrigerate until cool, at least 30 minutes.

Combine the orange juice, vinegar, wine, sesame oil, jalapeño, and ginger in a large mixing bowl. Whisk together thoroughly. Lay the smelt in a shallow glass or plastic dish and pour the marinade over the fish. Refrigerate overnight.

Serve with fresh lemon wedges and Parsley-Olive Sauce.

3 tablespoons good-quality olive oil

2 pounds fresh smelt, cleaned

1 cup flour

1 cup fresh orange juice

¼ cup white vinegar

¼ cup dry white wine

1 tablespoon Asian sesame oil

1 jalapeño pepper, diced

1 tablespoon finely chopped fresh ginger

1 lemon, cut into wedges

Parsley-Olive Sauce (see page 32)

Bok Choy-Wrapped Fish Terrine

Makes 15 ½-inch slices

4 tablespooons (½ stick) butter

1 cup finely chopped sweet
   white onion

¾ cup finely diced carrots

¾ cup finely chopped celery

¼ cup dry white wine

6-8 bok choy leaves, most of main
   stem removed

1 large red bell pepper

2 tablespoons vegetable oil

1 pound boneless and skinless white
   fish, such as bass, walleye, or cod

4 large eggs, lightly beaten

1 cup heavy cream

1 tablespoon chopped fresh tarragon

2 tablespoons stemmed fresh thyme

¼ cup trimmed and finely
   chopped scallions

1 tablespoon white pepper

2 ripe avocados, peeled, seeded,
   and thinly sliced

1 cucumber, peeled, seeded,
   and thinly sliced

1 pound salmon fillet, skinned

1 cup Red Pepper Sauce
   (recipe follows)

ONE MIGHT CONSIDER this light terrine for a picnic at the base of Katterskill Falls in upstate New York, where you can still see, intact from the nineteenth century, serifed initials engraved in stone by several Hudson River School painters. Frederic Church painted here. His house, Olana—now a grand museum—is only a few miles away, across the Hudson River.

The layering of the ingredients in this terrine creates an attractive, multicolored slice. Surrounded by Red Pepper Sauce and Avocado Mayonnaise, this terrine is particularly welcome after the scenic climb up the rocky Katterskill Creek to the falls.

The terrine should be refrigerated overnight before serving. It will keep for 6-7 days in the refrigerator.

Melt half the butter in a medium saucepan over medium-low heat and sauté the onions, carrots, and celery for 8-10 minutes, until soft. Add the white wine and reduce by one-half, about 5 minutes. Remove from the heat and set aside.

Bring a large pot of water to a boil, add salt, and blanch the bok choy leaves, 2-3 at a time, until they just wilt, about 30 seconds. Transfer to paper towels to drain.

Brush the bell pepper with vegetable oil and roast it over the flame of a gas burner, or place on a broiling pan 2-3-inches under the broiler. Roast on all sides until blackened. Transfer to a paper or plastic bag, seal, and set aside for about 10 minutes.

Preheat the oven to 325°F.

Puree the white fish in a food processor for 15-20 seconds, until finely chopped. Add the onion mixture and process for 20-30 seconds more, until thoroughly blended with the fish. Add the eggs and cream and process for another 5-10 seconds (do not whip the cream). With a rubber spatula, transfer the mousse to a large bowl. Add the tarragon, thyme, scallions, 1 teaspoon salt, and the pepper. Mix thoroughly, cover, and refrigerate until needed.

Peel away the blackened skin from the roasted pepper, cut in half, and scrape out the seeds and veins. Slice into 1-inch wide lengths and set aside.

Melt the remaining butter and brush it on the sides and bottom of a 5 x 9 x 3-inch loaf pan. Line the sides and bottom of the pan with the bok choy leaves, leaving generous edges hanging over the sides.

Place a layer of avocado slices on the bok choy leaves. With a rubber spatula, spread a half-inch layer of the mousse over the avocado. Place the red pepper strips on top of the mousse, then make a layer of cucumber slices. Lay the salmon fillet on top of the cucumbers. (You may have to trim the fillet to fit the shape of the pan; reserve any scraps for another dish.) The salmon will be the center of the terrine.

Repeat layers of avocado, mousse, red peppers, and cucumber until you fill the pan. Fold over the bok choy leaves to cover the terrine completely. Add more leaves if necessary. Cover with aluminum foil. Tap the terrine gently on the counter to eliminate air pockets.

Place a pan larger than the terrine in the oven and fill it half way with warm water. Place the terrine in the water and bake for about 1½ hours, or until a thermometer inserted in the center reads 130°F. Remove from the oven, discard the aluminum foil, and let cool for about 10 minutes.

Run a dull knife between the bok choy leaves and the pan on all sides. Invert the pan over a plate and run hot water over the bottom. Tap it with the handle of a knife to coax the terrine out onto the plate. Carefully pat dry and wrap in plastic wrap, and refrigerate for at least 1 hour.

To serve, cut the terrine into half-inch slices with a sharp knife. Place a slice on a plate and spoon some Red Pepper Sauce on one side and some Avocado Mayonnaise on the other. Sprinkle fresh salmon roe on top of the terrine and garnish with radicchio leaves and lemon slices.

1 cup Avocado Mayonnaise (recipe follows)

6 ounces fresh salmon roe

Radicchio leaves, for garnish

Fresh lemon slices, for garnish

To Drink:

For a refreshing afternoon drink, serve glasses of fresh lemonade spiked with a jigger of melon liqueur. Garnish with an aromatic sprig of fresh mint.

Red Pepper Sauce

Makes about 1 cup

2 large red bell peppers

1 tablespoon vegetable oil

2 tablespoons butter

1 small sweet white onion, finely chopped (about ½ cup)

1 medium carrot, shredded (about ½ cup)

1 teaspoon Trinidad masala (see Mail-Order Sources), cayenne, or chili powder

1 teaspoon salt

1 teaspoon freshly ground pepper

¼ cup chicken stock or sweet cream

THIS SAUCE CAN BE USED IN MANY WAYS. It is good over quail but goes nicely atop a piece of salmon, too. I have also used it as a base for soup by adding milk or more cream or chicken stock. It will keep frozen for up to 6 months.

If you do not want to roast your own peppers, use canned, roasted peppers. The Italian, Greek, and Spanish imports are best, but some can be bitter so you may want to add a tablespoon of honey or sugar as a sweetener.

Brush the peppers with oil and hold over the flame of a gas burner or outdoor grill with a skewer, or place on a broiling pan 2-3 inches under the broiler. Roast on all sides until blackened, about 10 minutes. Transfer to a paper or plastic bag, seal, and set aside for about 10 minutes.

Melt the butter in a medium sauté pan over medium heat. Add the onion, carrots, Trinidad masala, and salt and pepper. Sauté for about 10 minutes, until soft.

Remove the peppers from the bag, peel away all of the skin, cut into quarters and remove stems and veins. Combine with the onion mixture in the bowl of a food processor. Puree for 1 minute, then scrape down the sides with a rubber spatula. Pulse 5-6 times more. Add stock or cream and puree for about 2 minutes. Serve immediately or refrigerate for up to 2 days.

Avocado Mayonnaise

Makes about 2½ cups

1 cup ripe avocado, peeled and seeded (1 large or 2 small avocados)

2 cups mayonnaise

¼ cup finely chopped scallions

Juice of 1 lemon (about 2-3 tablespoons)

Salt and pepper, to taste

THIS COLORFUL MAYONNAISE IS DELICIOUS on the Apple-Smoked Roast Boar Sandwich (see page 114) or as a dip with nachos or chips. It will keep 3-4 days in the refrigerator.

Puree the avocado in a food processor until smooth, about 1 minute. Scrape down the sides with a rubber spatula and add the mayonnaise, scallions, lemon juice and salt and pepper (if using). Pulse 5-6 times, until the mixture is thoroughly blended. Transfer to a glass container, cover, and refrigerate.

Escabeche with Grilled Spring Onions

Serves 4 to 6

2 bunches large spring onions

2 pounds mixed firm-fleshed skinless white fish fillets (such as yellowtail, herring, mackerel, striped bass)

½ cup olive oil, plus extra for basting

1 cup lime juice

2 small plum tomatoes, seeded and diced

½ cup finely chopped red onion

1 small jalapeño pepper, seeded, deveined, and finely chopped

3 garlic cloves, finely chopped

2 tablespoons finely chopped fresh cilantro

½ teaspoon cayenne (optional)

½ teaspoon salt

1 tablespoon cracked black peppercorns

1 large head radicchio

Avocado slices and lime wedges for garnish

IN PUERTO ESCONDIDO in southern Mexico, the beachfront restaurants feature whatever was caught that day by local fishermen. We had one outstanding dish in several restaurants, varying of course by the hand of the cook. A regional specialty, escabeche always includes a variety of fish, onions, and most important, lime juice. A popular side dish served everywhere is grilled spring onions.

The following escabeche recipe includes a variety of fish—you can use most any firm-fleshed white fish (salt or freshwater). I recommend yellowtail, if you can get it. Do not confuse it with yellowfin tuna; the yellowtail is a Pacific member of the mackerel family. It is ideally suited for escabeche. As for the grilled spring onions, use the largest ones you can find because small ones are likely to dry out when grilled too long. I choose to grill the fish for this recipe (most escabeche recipes call for raw fish); it adds depth to the flavor. However, grill the fish briefly, leaving the interior raw.

Light a charcoal fire.

Trim the roots and about 2 inches of the green tops from the spring onions and set aside.

When the charcoal is gray and hot, brush the fish fillets and spring onions with olive oil and place them on the grate of the grill, making sure they are not touching. Grill 2-3 minutes, until they begin to char. Turn, baste, and grill 2-3 minutes more. Transfer the fish and scallions to a plate to cool for about 15 minutes.

In a large bowl combine ½ cup olive oil, the lime juice, tomatoes, onion, jalapeño, garlic, cilantro, cayenne, and salt and pepper. Set aside.

Cut the scallions into 1-inch lengths. Cut the fish into 1-inch chunks and add both to the olive oil mixture. Mix gently so the fish does not break apart, cover, and refrigerate for 2-3 hours.

Break apart the radicchio and place 3 or 4 four leaves in a circle on each plate. Remove the escabeche from the refrigerator and ladle equal portions over the radicchio with a slotted spoon, draining off most of the marinade.

Garnish with slices of avocado and wedges of lime.

To Drink:

Serve with one of Mexico's finest cervezas, with a piece of lime.

The Big One

Puerto Escondido, a stereotypically quiet fishing village on the Pacific coast of Mexico, lies about 200 miles north of the Guatemalan border. The area is less traveled than others along the coast and the village is not overdeveloped—yet. It didn't take long to arrange for a low-end fishing expedition on the high seas.

Jose, the young "captain," agreed to meet me early the next morning, and we settled on a reasonable fee. I convinced a kindred soul to come along—Martin Blazy, a fellow American I sipped a few beers with at the bar. Martin was at the concierge desk, somewhat bleary-eyed, at 4:30 A.M.

Jose's English was equal to my Spanish, so we gestured with hands a lot. But he was personable, quiet, and eager to cast off. The three of us dragged the heavy boat—a seventeen-foot wooden-hull vessel with a multicolored canvas awning supported by four shoddy two-by-fours—down the beach to the water.

Jose, I noticed, in the dim light of morning, had only one fifty-horse-power motor attached to his underequipped boat. It was connected to the largest plastic gas container I had ever seen, taking up most of the stern. Looking around the boat I noticed there was no radio. It was nothing Martin needed to know about, I decided.

The night before I had arranged for sandwiches and bottled water from the hotel restaurant. Jose took the stern, I was stationed in the center seat, and Martin selected a higher vantage point on the bow seat. By the time day had inched its way up, land was fading fast behind us, along with my passport, travelers checks, and sense of security.

"*Señor! Eso! Pescado! Eso!*" Jose was gesturing wildly to starboard. Swordfish were jumping all around the boat; we were motoring through the center of a large school. After fifteen minutes of anxious casting, retrieving, and casting, we were out of the school of crazed fish as suddenly as we'd thrust into it. We withdrew our lines and continued our journey to deeper and, we hoped, more fruitful fishing grounds.

At about ten or eleven I started to get fidgety. I could not see any land behind us and asked Martin if he thought we were out a bit too far.

"It seems we should be able to see land," I said tentatively, "but Jose must know where he's going, don't you think?" Martin agreed. We decided to eat lunch.

"*Señor!* Your line. *Rápido!* Much big *pescado muy grande!* Oh, my God!" So he did speak some English. I understood and threw out a huge popper, teasing it over the surface of the waves. It worked.

When the marlin slammed the lure, I was yanked down off my seat and smacked onto the deck, feet propped against the inside wall. The fish flew into the air like a turquoise rocket catapulted from the depths of the ocean. It twisted and gyrated, trying to rid itself of the biting steel caught in its mouth. It was pissed off; we were an intrusion on its territory. The fish continued to fight back, mysterious force, causing it to jump several more times high into the air.

"Reel! Reel, Señor! No slack. *Tirante!* Hold tight!" Jose pleaded. Martin reeled in his line, put aside his rod, and watched.

I scrambled back to my seat, while Jose strapped a rod holster around my waist that cut into my groin like a dull knife. Thirty minutes later my hands ached, my ass hurt, and my forearms had started to cramp. I would reel the line a little, hold tight so as not to allow any slack, reel in again, hold tight, and reel again. Within a short time the marlin had quit its acrobatics, so it wasn't as much fun. Every twenty minutes the fish dived toward the ocean floor so rapidly the reel screeched and nearly smoked from fiction. Jose periodically splashed water onto the reel and my hands to cool them while continuing his expert coaching. "Reel, *Señor!* Reel!"

The fish began diving deeper. I thought I'd give the line over to Jose, or that Martin might like to join the fun. Then I recalled a story by Ernest Hemingway, who had taken his three young boys deep-sea fishing off the coast of Key West. His son David hooked his first large fish, and his hands became bloodied, both feet blistered from pushing against the stern railing. When the blisters broke they bled too. Three hours later David was still fighting this fish. When it finally neared the boat, the line broke and the fish swam off. Yet Hemingway said he had seen grown men lose a fish without fighting half the battle David had. My hands weren't bleeding yet, but sweat poured off my forehead as I imagined Hemingway whispering in my ear, "Reel, you lazy sonafabitch,

keep reeling and don't give up, you miserable wimp."

Jose had taken to whittling and sharpening what looked like a piece of two-by-four with his machete. Fishermen here make a considerable commission selling sportsmen's catches to local restaurants; he wasn't going to let dinner get away if he could help it.

I turned to Martin. "I hope he's not going to be too disappointed when I tell him that I don't want to kill this fish, that I want to release it."

"You do?"

"Yes. There's a decline in the world's population of billfish because of sport-fishing. They're becoming endangered." I cranked the reel, huffing and puffing. "If they continue feeding these fish to us tourists in beachfront restaurants, there won't be any billfish left in Mexico." My hands slipped in my own hot sweat.

"I don't think you can convey that to Jose," Martin said. "He's just untied the anchor rope and made a lasso out of it."

More than two hours had gone by since the struggle began, and I could tell by the amount of line rewound onto the reel that the fish must be near the surface. It was. The line moved horizontally across the water, then slowly zigzagged toward the boat. Martin let out the first exclamation. "Jeeeessus, would you look at that," he whispered.

"I don't see anything," I said, scanning the water.

"Right in front of us, down about six feet. It's as long as the boat!" Martin was now as excited as Jose, who was close to jumping into the water, native spear in one hand, lasso in the other.

"Where?" I asked. "I see some color but I don't see the—Yes, now I see!" I caught a glimpse of a bright turquoise streak passing just alongside the boat.

Mild-mannered Jose made the sign of the cross and jumped over my seat to get higher up on the bow, bouncing the two-by-four off the back of my head in the process.

Then it happened. The rod in my hand suddenly wasn't tethered to anything. There was no tension. Only slack line. The mighty fish had broken off, the hook slipped away from its thin lip. A seagull squawked. Martin continued to scan the water. Jose stood on his stern seat, a crestfallen Ishmael.

Do you know the expression on people's faces when they bet big and lose? There is none. It is void. The three of us looked as if we had been lobotomized. We were still, I'm sure, for many minutes. No one spoke. There was no sound except the seagull. Jose remained mesmerized, fractured, disbelieving, till I set the rod down and said, "Should we go in now?" The trip to Puerto Escondido was long.

Back at the beach a Texas fisherman was being photographed alongside his catch, a five- or six-foot sailfish propped against the breaker. A small crowd had gathered.

"How long did it take to bring in your fish?" I asked the Texan.

"Oh, about twenty, maybe thirty minutes, I suppose. Good fightin' fish," he said proudly.

"What do you think it weighs?" I asked.

His "captain" was standing nearby and overheard our conversation. "About forty or fifty kilos," he said.

"How long is it?" I inquired.

"Oh, eight, maybe ten feet," the Texan quickly responded. "Y'all catch anything?"

"Ah, yeah, I—guess I did."

"Don't sound like you know."

"Mine got away."

"Tough luck, son." We were about the same age. "Y'all come with me next time. I'll show you the hot spots."

I asked José to tell his colleague how big my marlin had been. "A marlin as big as the boat," Martin interjected.

The two captains spoke in an animated fashion for several minutes. Jose's friend's dark eyes widened. "How long you fight your fish, señor?" he asked.

"More than a couple of hours, maybe two and a half or so," I told him.

"A very large fish, señor. And you lost him?"

"Sí," I responded. "Sí."

After a few more minutes of discussion, Jose's friend turned to me and said, "Your fish, he may have weighed about 150 kilos, maybe more."

"That's more than 300 pounds," Martin breathed.

"Si, señor," the skipper said. "You caught a big fish. Very big. You must have been very far out," He added. Jose caught my eye and looked away.

Marinated Kippered Herring

HERRING'S DELICATE WHITE FLESH has been enjoyed by various cultures since the beginning of time. Their vast territory extends from the Norwegian Sea to the North Sea to the Irish Sea and across the Atlantic to the eastern seaboard of North America.

When cleaning the herring, save both the hard roe (orange, also referred to as the eggs) and the soft roe (white, also referred to as "milt"). Use the hard roe for another dish or gently sauté with butter and white wine to serve on the side with the herring fillets. The soft roe will be used as below.

The herring may be refrigerated for at least 2 weeks or frozen for up to 8 months.

24 small to medium fresh herring, cleaned and headed, ½ cup soft roe (milt) reserved

¼ cup white vinegar

¼ cup sugar

1 tablespoon coarse-grain (kosher) salt

6 bay leaves

6 tablespoons pickling spices or crab boil

1 large white onion, about ½ pound

1 large lemon, thinly sliced

¾ cup Dijon mustard

¾ cup mayonnaise

¼ cup chopped fresh dill

Lemon Slices

Parsley sprigs

Light a charcoal fire in a backyard smoker (see page 180).

When the charcoal is gray and hot, lay the herring on the top grate of the smoker, cover, and smoke for 2 hours, turning once. Replenish charcoal and wood chips as needed. Remove the herring to a platter.

Meanwhile, rinse the soft roe in cold water through a small wire strainer. Mash it with a fork or spoon in a small mixing bowl. Add 1 cup of water and the vinegar, sugar, salt, bay leaves, and spices, and whisk together.

Peel and slice the onion into thin (⅛-inch to ¼-inch) slices and separate into rings. Place one layer of herring in a large glass or ceramic dish, then add a layer of onions and a layer of lemon slices, repeating until you have filled the container. Pour the soft roe mixture into the container, covering the fish completely. Cover and refrigerate for at least 2 days. Mix the mustard, mayonnaise, and dill. Serve with the herring and garnish with parsley sprigs and lemon slices.

Warm Smoked Duck, Wild Rice & Oyster Salad

Serves 6 to 8

4 duck breasts, about 2 pounds

½ cup walnut oil

2 tablespoons balsamic vinegar

1 teaspoon Dijon mustard

Salt

1 teaspoon cracked black peppercorns

¾ pound wild rice

1 tablespoon olive oil

12-16 shucked fresh oysters (2 per person)

1 tablespoon brandy

6 scallions, finely chopped

⅓ cup hazelnuts, skinned and finely chopped

½ cup finely chopped Jerusalem artichokes, kohlrabi, or jicama

1 cup cleaned and stemmed watercress

Orange zest and diced red bell pepper for garnish

BEFORE CAROLE CLARK—my partner at both Konkapot and Charleston Restaurants—and I began our stint in the restaurant world, we came up with this recipe one evening at her home. I believe the combination was originally Carole's idea.

I had planned to smoke a duck in the stone fireplace. We had some fresh oysters so I hung them up in the flue, tied into cheese-cloth bags, along with the duck. As many regular customers from both restaurants may recall, we served this salad for many years, especially on New Year's Eve.

If you smoke the duck breast and legs, you can serve Smoked Hoisin Duck Legs for dinner and this salad the next day.

This recipe does not call for smoked oysters, but if you wish, you can wrap shucked oysters in cheesecloth and smoke them at the same time you smoke the ducks (only for about 45 minutes).

Serve this salad as a main-course lunch for a picnic or on a sunny fall day.

Light a charcoal fire in a backyard smoker. (See page 180.)

Wash and pat dry the duck breasts and trim the excess skin and fat.

When the charcoal is gray and hot, lay the breasts on the wire rack over the wood chips. Cover and smoke for 1 ½-2 hours, until the meat feels firm when poked with your finger, maintaining the internal temperature of the smoker at 250-300°F. Add charcoal and wood chips as needed. Remove the smoked breasts from the grill, cool, wrap in plastic wrap, and refrigerate. (The recipe can be prepared ahead up to this point and kept in the refrigerator for up to 2 days.)

To make the dressing, combine the walnut oil, vinegar, mustard, salt, and pepper in a large bowl and whisk together thoroughly. Transfer to a serving container and set aside.

Rinse the wild rice and place in a medium saucepan, then add enough water to cover the wild rice completely by half an inch. Cover, bring to a boil, reduce the heat to low, and simmer for 40-45 minutes, until rice is soft and not crunchy. Cover and set aside to keep warm.

Remove the smoked duck breast from the refrigerator and cut into bite-size pieces. Set aside.

Heat the olive oil in a small sauté pan over medium-high heat. Add the oysters and sauté for about 1 minute, until slightly firm, then add brandy, scallions, hazelnuts, and duck. Sauté for 2-3 minutes, until warmed, remove the pan from heat, cover, and set aside.

Combine the wild rice with the Jerusalem artichokes in a large bowl along with the oyster mixture. Toss together with walnut-oil dressing, or serve dressing on the side.

Arrange the watercress neatly on plates and using tongs or forks, place equal servings of the salad over the watercress.

Sprinkle each plate with orange zest and diced red pepper and serve.

To Drink:

Guigal's white Côtes du Rhône, from France is less well known than its reds, but this elegant wine will hold up to the smoked duck and not overpower the delicate oyster flavors.

Or try a California white burgundy, perhaps from Mirassou Vineyard in California. It is inexpensive yet dry, and compatible with oysters and wild rice.

Wild Duck Terrine with Wild Mushrooms & Dried Apricots

Makes 15 ½-inch slices

1 pound leg meat and scraps from duck or pheasant, ground or finely chopped, or 1 pound ground turkey

¼ cup maple syrup

2 tablespoons crème de cassis

3 tablespoons dry vermouth

3 large eggs

½ cup finely chopped dried apricots

2 teaspoons finely chopped fresh tarragon

2 teaspoons stemmed fresh thyme

2 teaspoons coarsely chopped fresh parsley

1 teaspoon ground nutmeg

½ teaspoon cayenne

1 teaspoon salt

2 tablespoons cracked black peppercorns

Breast meat from 2 wild ducks, 1 large pheasant, or 1 moulard duck breast, about 1 pound of meat

4 bay leaves

1 cup chopped fresh wild mushrooms (about 2 ounces) or ½ cup (½ ounce) dried mushrooms, chopped

½ cup dry sherry

THE NUMBER OF DUCKS NEEDED FOR THIS recipe will depend upon the size and type of duck. You will certainly need more breast meat if you have a wood duck than, say, a mallard because of its smaller size.

Sea ducks would be fine for this recipe, but you may want to soak them in a weak solution of salt and vinegar overnight if you do not like the fishy-liver taste of these ducks, which some people object to.

If you plan to serve this from an attractive porcelain terrine, scrape off the top layer of bacon, clean the edges, and cut slices directly out of the container. If you use a loaf pan, you will want to remove the terrine from the pan and trim away all the bacon before slicing.

Serve with Olive-Parsley Sauce (see page 32) or a coarse-grain mustard and croutons.

Substitute pheasant breasts for duck breasts if you wish. If you have neither wild duck nor pheasant, you may be able to obtain moulard duck breasts from your butcher.

In a large mixing bowl combine the ground meat with the maple syrup, cassis, vermouth, eggs, apricots, tarragon, thyme, parsley, nutmeg, cayenne, salt, and pepper. Stir together well. Press the duck breasts into the mix, submerging completely. Press in the bay leaves. Cover and refrigerate at least 2 hours.

Soak the mushrooms in the sherry for about 30 minutes. Drain the mushrooms, retaining the liquid.

Preheat the oven to 325°F.

Melt the butter in a small sauté pan and cook the onion and mushrooms over medium heat for about 6-8 minutes, until the onion is translucent. Remove the pan from the heat and set aside.

Remove the ground meat mixture from the refrigerator. Take out the duck breasts and bay leaves, and discard the bay leaves. Add the onion mixture to the ground meat mixture and stir together well.

Slice the duck breasts lengthwise into ⅛-inch julienne. Set aside. Line the bottom and sides of a porcelain terrine (approximately 4 x 7 x 3 inches) or a large loaf pan (5 x 9 x 3 inches) with the bacon slices. With a rubber spatula, spoon a ¼-inch layer of the ground meat on the bottom of the terrine. Lay strips of duck breast on top of the ground meat. Cover the duck breast with another ¼-inch layer of ground meat. Alternate layers of duck breast with ground meat until you have filled the terrine. (Any excess may be frozen to fry as breakfast patties or hors d'oeuvres.) Cover with a layer of bacon. Tightly crimp a piece of aluminum foil over the container. Gently tap the terrine on the counter to settle the mix and eliminate air pockets. Place a deep baking pan larger than the terrine in the oven and fill it half way with warm water. Set the terrine in the pan. Bake for 1 ¾ hours. Remove, loosen foil, and place a heavy weight on top of the foil to press out excess fat (I keep a clean brick wrapped in 2 layers of heavy-duty aluminum foil just for this purpose). Set aside to cool about 1 hour.

To remove the terrine from a loaf pan, remove the foil, and run a dull knife all around the inside edges of the pan. Invert the pan over a plate and run hot water over the bottom of the pan. Tap the bottom of the pan with the handle of a knife to coax it out onto the plate. Carefully pat dry, slice away the bacon, and wrap in plastic wrap.

The terrine should age for several days in the refrigerator before serving. It may be frozen for up to 2 months.

2 tablespoons butter
½ cup finely chopped white onion
½ pound lean bacon
Olive-Parsley Sauce (see page 32)

To Drink:

Catherine and Pascal Rollet earn high marks for their Pouilly-Fuissé, Domaine de la Chapelle Vieilles Vignes. The 1993 is an excellent, understated, round white with honey, pear, lemon, and melon flavors that will keep well because of its high acidity. It is a good-value white Burgundy that is a fine accompaniment to a slice of duck terrine at a summer picnic.

Or try one of the newer stars, a Pinot Gris from Oregon. WillaKenzie offers this delicately oaked and well-balanced cousin of Italy's Pinot Grigio.

Olive-Parsley Sauce

Makes 1¼ cups

½ cup + 1 tablespoon good-quality
olive oil

¼ cup pine nuts

4 cups chopped fresh parsley

12 medium green olives, pitted

6 garlic cloves

1 tablespoon Dijon mustard

½ teaspoon cayenne

1 tablespoon lemon juice

I HAVE USED THIS SAUCE to baste roast leg of boar, to coat steaks before grilling, as a sandwich spread with prosciutto, and to accompany pâté.

But Olive-Parsley Sauce is even more versatile: if you add 3-4 anchovies to the puree you have an excellent sauce to accompany fish. Baste the fish with the sauce when grilling or baking and serve more on the side, or swirl a tablespoon or two into a fish soup. It also tastes great on a sardine sandwich.

This sauce may be refrigerated for up to 6 days, but it is best served fresh.

Heat 1 tablespoon of the oil in a small sauté pan over medium-high heat. Add the pine nuts, stir to coat with the oil, and continue stirring until the nuts are browned, about 1½ minutes. Be watchful—they burn easily. Remove quickly and transfer to paper towels to drain.

Puree the pine nuts, parsley, olives, garlic, mustard, and cayenne in a food processor for about 1 minute. Scrape down the sides of the bowl with a spatula, process again for a few seconds, and drizzle the lemon juice and ½ cup olive oil through the feed tube simultaneously until completely integrated into a smooth paste (you will have to pour the oil at a faster rate then the lemon juice).

Serve immediately, or cover and refrigerate.

Roughing It

The two-phase alarm goes off each morning shortly before sunup. The first part is the gentle staccato of a loon whistling out on the lake. The second is the more jarring, unmistakable thunk of a piece of firewood being split too near the head of my tent.

I can see my breath as I scramble to dress within the warmth of my down sleeping bag. From outside, I hear the crunch of frozen ground giving way under pac boots as the early risers tend the breakfast fire. I shiver and stall until I hear the coffee boiling.

Most every fall around this time, a group of friends and I travel north to Ontario to hunt and fish. We fish for coho and chinook salmon, rainbow, brown, and lake trout. We hunt freely for ducks, geese, rabbit, and ruffed grouse. Dropped off at this spectacular wilderness juncture by a Lake Superior fisherman in his converted tugboat, we unload our three canoes, 1,500 pounds of gear, and two cases of good wine, vintage port, and a bottle of French apple brandy, calvados. We are picked up seven to ten days later, depending on the weather and the captain's fishing schedule—or, more likely, his whim.

The highlight of our trip is preparing and cooking smoky meals, often punctuated by howling coyotes and sometimes the arrival of the beginnings of a nasty autumn storm blowing off Lake Superior. We set up camp on the lee side of sandy white beaches, thirty yards from the world's largest body of fresh water. Evenings often reward us with crimson sunsets over the lake, flickering through the dense mix of black birch, red maple, and Norway pine. Spectacular displays of aurora borealis in the northern night sky entertain us as we prepare to dine on delicacies fetched from the waters and woods of Canada's rugged wilderness. Here I learned not to mind having my feet slosh about inside a pair of wet boots in bone-chilling weather for an entire day. Or more.

Day one is set aside for laying out the campsite, setting up tents (including one for provisions), and organizing the gear. Erecting the sheltered kitchen and living area, adjacent to the all-important fire, is paramount. Tall poles are cut and notched. Clear plastic is rolled out and lashed down. A makeshift fold-back awning is tied over the fire area in case of heavy rain or snow. (It has snowed or rained heavily every trip.) Within a day the site looks as if it has been inhabited by a small scouting party for weeks.

The first sign of settling in is a pair of wet socks hung to dry. Cooking paraphernalia is spread out. I prepare my condiments, sharpen knives, and set up the portable outdoor smoker, a primitive structure I constructed on a previous trip that has since yielded many an enjoyable dining experience.

A typical day at camp centers around the communal fire, perpetually aglow not only for chilly fingers and toes but to keep the cast-iron Dutch oven simmering with stew of the day. Or should I say of the hour; the recipe is mostly the catch at any given moment. There is one steadfast rule for the stew pot: no mix of meat and fish. This technique is our contemporary woodsman's version of *scottiglia*, a traditional Tuscan dish assembled by villagers, who would stroll past the vast, communal vat and toss in their contribution.

On the shores of Lake Superior, each day's menu changes according to weather and the gathering ability of each sportsman—the shopping list, as it were. Shots from the beach alert those in camp that mallard duck may have to be plucked; gunshots from the forest signal another brace of grouse to prepare for the spit. And you never know what species of Salmonidae will be caught upriver, at the base of the falls.

The appreciation of otherwise unobtainable wild tastes has been a significant evolution in our culinary forays. Two decades ago, when I first went camping with these men, I kept quiet as we hastily loaded supermarket pushcarts with jars of Tang, powdered milk, white bread, peanut butter, jelly, and endless packages of powdered soups, mixes, and other junk. I suffered greatly that year. The following year I demanded $100 per man and did the shopping.

Our group has learned to augment the challenging wild menus with vegetables from bulging gardens, herbs, spices, wild rice, dried pasta (for barren spells), tomato paste, garlic, and dried chilies, hauled with some effort into the great Canadian outdoors. And I never forget to pack cardamom seeds to add to the coffee, cooked over a wood fire in a blackened enamel pot and laced with calvados—French cowboy coffee at a Canadian fireside.

Over the years our closely knit group has become an organization of responsible, environmentally aware, culinary-minded sportsmen who enjoy the resulting camaraderie. We still don't shower for days on end, are constantly disheveled, unshaven, and dangerous- and ill-mannered-looking when viewed from afar: shotguns and black powder rifles propped against trees among ever-present wet socks, curing salmon, and drying long underwear may not convey a sense of refinement. Actually, however, we are all somewhat rational, well mannered, and mostly in control of our senses.

The ventures are not uniformly productive. Weather and water conditions are critical to the migration and spawning of fish; we may not be there when they run the river. Ruffed grouse appear and disappear in seven-year cycles; we have visited Canada on "off" years and come up empty-handed. Indian Summers can affect waterfowl's annual habits and thus our bag limits. It is the adaptive sportsman who dines fireside with satisfaction.

On any day in camp there is a primary job—keeping the fire supplied with wood for the cookpot and for warmth. Group activities are spontaneous: the fly-tying center materializes when someone discovers a pattern that is producing fish; a frenzy of shaggymane mushroom picking occurs when they're found growing at the river's edge.

Life is lazy and uncomplicated at the 47th parallel,

there, not far from the sunken ship the *Edmund Fitzgerald* immortalized in song by Gordon Lightfoot. The air is crisp in the morning light. Our stays have been warmly fulfilling, in spite of frosty mornings and frigid appendages.

At any time one might find, suspended too low over the entrance to the polypropylene kitchen, two or three rabbits, five or six grouse, a black duck, and several salmon, the fish already injected with a cure and aging in the perfect natural refrigeration. The smoker is tended throughout the day so no morsel of wild food is oversmoked, and the canvas cover is wetted periodically so our bounty does not end in flames. Salmon and lake trout smoke sweetly over green maple, or my favorite wood up there, black birch.

It is easy to become spoiled eating fish that has been cured, smoked, cooked, and consumed within hours of being caught—in other words, fresh.

A memorable meal, and one of my favorites, is spit-roasted ruffed grouse, basted with olive oil, slightly charred by the flames of a crackling fire. Six or eight birds tied tightly to a hefty green sapling are bathed in white wine, oil, lemon juice, and fresh herbs, rubbed vigorously with a freshly cut tomato, and left to soak up the flavors. Wild rice and large chunks of buttered zucchini or butternut squash roasted over the fire make satisfying accompaniments. And it's hard to resist a smoked-salmon appetizer. I've even noticed a side of salmon disappear mysteriously after dinner.

The wine: ah, only noble reds should be consumed with game in the great outdoors. And we brook no shortage of vintages to select from. Room temperature, unfortunately is a problem. Autumn Canadian air is unpredictable, has intermittent drafts, and is a far cry from the constant 50 degrees of a reputable wine cellar, and snow can surround and cover our Wine Cellar by the Lake. Ingenuity is called for.

At first my comrades thought me a bit daffy, but after a while the sight of the neck of a wine bottle protruding from my down vest became welcome come dinnertime. This tactic can be awkward while fly-fishing; but it's curiously like the nineteenth-century British teaching technique of holding a book firmly under your arm while practice-casting, a lesson in keeping the arm close to the body. After running experiments on raising the temperature of a bottle of wine approximately 15 degrees, I can verify that you can do it with minimal harm—even to a delicate 1982 Margaux.

A marriage of delicious matched tastes and lasting memories took place in western Ontario one fall evening under some classic fireworks courtesy of the arctic northern lights. The prelude was a butterflied, grilled black duck smothered in sautéed shaggymane. Lightly smoked, spit-roasted, ruffed grouse and a 1970 Château Pichon Lalande, both consumed at their proper temperatures, sealed the delicious union.

As the chilly night set in, we gathered nearer the embers to toast ourselves with calvados cowboy coffee. The port would have to wait for another evening.

Sautéed Big Game Heart with Chanterelles

Serves 2

¼ ounce dried or 1 ounce fresh chanterelles or oyster mushrooms

1 ounce Cognac (omit if using fresh mushrooms)

2 tablespoons butter

½ teaspoon plus 2 tablespoons canola oil

¼ medium white onion, finely chopped (about ¼ cup)

½ cup unsalted veal or chicken stock

2 tablespoons fresh blood (if available)

8 ounces venison, caribou, moose, elk, or other big game heart, thinly sliced

3 tablespoons pumpkin seeds

4-6 radicchio leaves

AT CHARLESTON RESTAURANT, one regular customer, who knew I enjoyed wines, often brought me great bottles from a restaurant estate he had bought. When fresh game was available, and I knew Jerry was in the dining room, I often surprised him with a special dish—Canada goose breast, a wild duck, or a big game heart, which he particularly enjoyed. We could not sell wild game (no United States restaurant is allowed to unless the meat is FDA inspected) but nothing prevented me from giving it to a friend. One evening I prepared a dish of sautéed venison heart, much to Jerry's delight.

Soak the dried mushrooms in the Cognac mixed with 2 tablespoons of water for about 30 minutes. (If using fresh mushrooms, merely chop and set aside.)

Melt the butter with ½ teaspoon oil in a medium saucepan over medium heat. Add the onion and sauté for 6-8 minutes, until translucent. Add the stock and blood. Simmer about 5 minutes, then add the heart with the mushrooms and their liquid. Cover and simmer for about 15 minutes, or until the meat is tender. Remove the cover and reduce the liquid for another 5 minutes.

While the meat is cooking, heat the remaining 2 tablespoons of oil in a heavy sauté pan over medium heat. Add the pumpkin seeds, turn the heat down to low, and stir constantly. The seeds will begin to brown and pop like popcorn. Stir or shake the pan, keeping the pan covered as much as possible or the seeds will end up everywhere. Remove the seeds when toasty brown, in about 2 minutes, and blot on a paper towel.

Remove the heart from the saucepan and slice thin.

Place the radicchio leaves on 2 plates, place half of the heart slices over each, and ladle some of the sauce over the top.

Game Pâté

Yields about 24 slices, ¾ inch thick

PÂTÉ SHOULD ALWAYS be aged. With 1-3 weeks of aging in the refrigerator, it will only get better. It can be frozen for up to 6 months.

I prefer coarsely ground meat, but you can grind the meat finer or even use the metal blade in a food processor to create a smooth pâté. Serve with Dijon mustard and brown or pumpernickel bread.

Using a meat grinder attachment of a mixer, grind the two meats and liver together (or have your butcher grind them for you). In a large bowl combine the meat, apricots, pecans, garlic, eggs, brandy, cream, cinnamon, cloves, cardamom, pepper, and salt. Mix with your hands or a large spoon, slowly incorporating the flour until thoroughly mixed. Cover and refrigerate overnight.

Preheat the oven to 425°F. Set a large baking pan on the middle shelf of the oven and fill half way with water.

Line the insides of two 5 x 9 x 3-inch loaf pans on the bottom and sides with the bacon. Add the pâté mixture. Cover with more strips of bacon and then with heavy aluminum foil. Set inside the larger baking pan, and bake for 2½ hours. Check the water level from time to time and add more if necessary.

Remove the loaf pans from the oven. Loosen the foil but do not remove. Place heavy vegetable cans or clean bricks wrapped in aluminum foil on top of each pan to push out excess fat while it cools. Set in a cool place for at least 1 hour and then refrigerate overnight.

The next day, remove the pâté by running a dull knife around the inside of the pans. Invert the pan over a plate and run hot water over the bottom of the pan. Tap the bottom of the pan with the handle of a knife to coax it out onto the plate. Carefully pat dry and wrap in plastic wrap. Age in the refrigerator for 1-3 weeks.

Serve with Dijon mustard and brown or pumpernickel bread.

¼ pound venison, caribou, or other big game meat, ground

1¾ pound fatty ground pork

1 pound ground duck, goose, chicken, or any poultry liver

½ cup dried apricots

⅓ cup coarsely chopped pecans, pistachios, hazelnuts, or macadamia nuts

⅓ cup finely chopped garlic cloves

4 eggs, beaten

½ cup brandy

½ cup heavy cream

½ teaspoon cinnamon

½ teaspoon ground cloves

1 teaspoon ground cardamom

2 tablespoons freshly ground black pepper

½ teaspoon salt

⅓ cup flour

1 pound fatty bacon

Trout, Shad, Walleye, Northern Pike

& Other Fish

Sautéed Trout with Morels & Spring Onions

Serves 4

2 tablespoons butter

6 small wild spring onions, finely chopped (or ½ cup chopped scallions or chives)

4 whole brook trout or 2 large rainbows, heads removed

5 medium-size fresh morels, thinly sliced (or ½ ounce dried mushrooms, soaked in water or sherry for 25 minutes)

2 tablespoons dry white vermouth or dry white wine

2 lemons, cut into wedges

To Drink

Trout goes well with a not-too-oaky French Chardonnay and you can never go wrong with Georges DuBoeuf, a reasonably priced white burgundy that is easy to find.

For a step up from the Duboeuf there's the reliable Louis Latour's Mâcon-Lugny, Les Genevrières. Delicate yet complex and well balanced, this Chardonnay tastes far better than one would think for the price.

WILD TROUT CAN BE DELICATE and delicious if they have not been recently dumped into a stream or lake from a hatchery, in which case they taste like the feed pellets they eat. It can take up to a few months to filter out the flavor of man-made food.

I tend not to fillet small fish, believing that you lose valuable meat in doing so. I also think that cooking fish with the bone results in more flavor.

If you cannot locate wild spring onions you can substitute either small scallions or chives. Wild onions look like scallions or garlic, popping up about 4-6 inches high, and tend to grow in thin patches in fields or in grassy areas.

Serve with home fries or hash brown potatoes and asparagus. If you can find it, try purple asparagus; it is quite flavorful.

Melt the butter in a large cast-iron skillet over medium heat. Add the onions and sauté for 6-8 minutes, until translucent. Add the trout and cook until the flesh is white, not translucent, about 5 minutes on each side depending upon the thickness of the fish (the flesh should reach 145°F. on a thermometer inserted into the thickest part of the trout). When you turn the fish, add the morels (if using dried mushrooms, add their juices). Stir occasionally.

Transfer the trout to a cutting board and remove the backbones (see page 180). Deglaze the pan with the vermouth or wine.

When serving, pour the deglazed juices over the fish. Squeeze fresh lemon juice over the trout and morels and serve immediately.

Dossier Lake

awa—They liked the name of the town so much they named it twice!" said my guide at Sault Ste. Marie, Ontario's municipal fish hatchery—when I told him where I was headed next. The man clearly relished his wit. But actually, *wawa* is Ojibway for wild goose, which he must have known and I had learned.

It was very warm—hot, really—when I pitched my tent at Oski-Wawa Campground. I first camped the spectacularly scenic region along the coast of Lake Superior 155 miles north of Sault Ste. Marie more than fifteen years ago, and it was after nine by the time I finished setting up camp. I had driven all day and it was too late to unpack cooking gear, so I headed into town. I knew the cuisine would be lake trout or walleye. Either would be fine with me. I always enjoy freshwater fish, and these would be fresh.

So after a walleye dinner at the Viking Restaurant I started back for camp. This northern latitude in June remains peculiarly bright till 11 P.M., and from a high ridge at the edge of town I saw a bunch of cars parked near a tourist information booth alongside a two-story-high statue of a Canada goose, the *wawa* of Wawa. At the same time, I began to smell burning conifers. I stopped, grabbed my camera, and joined the crowd to watch smoke billowing from a nearby valley.

"It looks like half the town turned out," someone said. "That's because there's no hockey on TV tonight," someone responded. A low greenish-orange veil hung in the valley, eerie, movielike. I took some photographs and lingered awhile, till I felt the weight of a long day and the invitation of a soft sleeping bag. The next day I was to meet a float plane at 11 A.M. for a five-day fishing trip on a secluded lake deep in the Ontario "bush," so I drove back to camp and turned in.

In the morning as I was packing my gear, the owner of the campground passed by and asked if I knew how close the forest fire had come. I was surprised to learn it had been burning within a couple of miles of where I had slept so soundly. Before leaving to meet the plane I toured the devastation with Joel Cooper, the region's spokesman for the Ministry of Natural Resources. He said there were more than one hundred forest fires reported that day and more than three hundred ablaze in the province.

Just before leaving home I'd had another near-brush with disaster; a tornado that cost three lives and millions of dollars in damage blew its 200 mph winds across a road I had passed just five minutes earlier. I was boarding a small bush plane in an hour. Should I worry?

I drove to Hawk Air, the carrier for my fly-in expedition, 12 miles north of Wawa. The company operates three planes; I was directed to the smaller Cesna being fueled. Two people are allowed one hundred pounds each in gear and provisions, so I packed whatever I wanted and no one said anything as everything, including two bottles of wine and plenty of cooking supplies, got loaded in ahead of me. Crawling feet-first into the passenger seat, I wondered whether it would be possible to extricate myself from the position.

Dossier Lake—pronounced "dough-sure" in Ontario—is one of twenty-two lakes in which Hawk Air drops off fishermen in summer and hunters in fall. There are no roads into the most remote camps, and no man could walk through the surrounding brush and forest. Hawk Air would retrieve me five days later.

The pilot wasn't talkative—not nervous, I hoped, just tired. "I do this all day long," he informed me. Having been in a service profession and in contact with many people each day, I understood his silence. I was happy to let him concentrate on flying, anyway.

Picking out Dossier from among the dozens of lakes scattered below us, the pilot set the Cesna down on the water flawlessly.

"You've done this before," I commented, breaking the silence.

"I've been in here about thirty times this year," he said coolly. And it was only June.

"You'll be back, right?" I waved as the plane drifted away from the dock 15 minutes later.

My cabin was new, nestled among tall jack pines, mountain ash, and old white cedar, the bark from which early fur traders had used to roof their forts. A large bay window let in too much light and sun, overlooking the south and westerly side of the horseshoe-shaped lake purportedly rich with speckled trout.

It was unusually hot, and the log cabin had only a few small screens and no screen door. After settling in and tying up fishing gear for later use, I doused myself with insect repellent and started to change into shorts. I never made it: there was no one around for miles, I realized; who would care if I wore shorts or didn't? So I didn't.

During the hottest part of the next few sweltering days I wore no clothes. Wind blowing through your . . . toes is exhilarating, unexpected, liberating. I had to duck for cover two or three times when bush planes flew by just over the treetops, but I became acclimated to the routine and enjoyed the newfound freedom. I even stopped assuming the forest was full of voyeurs. I was truly alone. Then the bugs introduced themselves.

The Ontario woods insect kingdom is enormous. And territorial. Moose flies, new to me and aptly named, own any airspace they choose. Horseflies buzz relentless concentric circles around your head, landing frequently to refuel. Mosquitoes are everywhere it's calm: the cabin, the porch, the dock, around the boat. Black flies prefer morning and evening dinner, with many small courses—grazing, as it were. "No-se-ums" are vampirish; they love you best when you try to sleep.

The insects had consistent biting times, and I adapted to their schedules, suffering greatly before learning who really ran the woods. Each day I juggled my activities: applying insect repellent, writing, alternating brands of insect repellent, dodging planes, putting on clothes, drawing, taking off clothes, and fishing. When the onslaught was the worst I wore a buttoned-up long-sleeved shirt, a hat, pants, and socks, keeping available epidermis to a minimum in temperatures I later learned hovered well over 100 degrees. But the rest of the day, clad only in insect repellent I caught speckled trout. Many fine trout.

Back home speckled trout is much the same as brook trout but up here the meat is bright orange, like salmon, and as good eating as any trout or salmon. The largest ones—one and a half pounds or so—linger near the bottom, so I tied on a split-shot weight ahead of a streamer, a Mickey Finn, or most anything with red or white and trolled deep. I caught several large trout with the setup.

The first day on Dossier was miserably hot and after torturously heating up the cabin while cooking dinner, I decided to prepare the following evening's meal early the next morning, while it was still cool. I developed a dish of cold pasta with speckled trout, turned out to be the highlight of my many meals at the lake. The bottle of Beaujolais I managed to bring with me, refreshingly chilled, paired well with my cold pasta that night on the dock, just before twilight.

Little friends from the wild hung around camp, including an aggressively hungry chipmunk that chewed his way through the screen as fast as I could tape them over; two black-and-white loons appearing regularly each morning; two squawking seagulls that assisted in cleaning the dock after I filleted fish; and two rabbits that skipped from the woods each day to sit brazenly near as I sketched. The wildlife companionship was a comfort I looked forward to.

Then several days later the temperature and humidity dropped considerably, the clothes went back on, and three canoeists paddled by my sanctuary—and stopped. If they had appeared twenty-four hours earlier, the father, his two sons, and I would all have been embarrassed. The closet nudist returned to his closet.

My new neighbors were paddling a Voyageurs route, the Canadian water version of the Appalachian Trail. It became apparent they, too, were interested in privacy; they camped at the far end of the lake. Each day we would wave and chat a bit between boats. I told them what spots, flies, and lures I had found most effective. I didn't need to tell them about insect repellent; they were Canadians, well educated on insect life in the bush.

If there'd been fewer insects and a cellular phone that worked across mountains, I would have called Hawk Air and delayed my return. Swatting aside, these were tranquil days of fishing, drawing, writing, and reading, a time I was loathe to relinquish. But when the pilot arrived as planned, the cabin was secured and my gear piled high on the dock, with me alongside, fully dressed.

Grilled Trout In Foil

Serves 4

1 tablespoon canola or peanut oil

4 tablespoons pumpkin seeds or pine nuts

4 1-pound whole rainbow trout or boned fillets of salmon

8 tablespoons (½ cup) butter

20 chives

20 garlic chives (optional)

1 large spring onion, peeled and quartered, about 1 pound, or 8 scallions

1 medium tomato, quartered

4 teaspoons ground cumin

2 teaspoons salt (or to taste)

2 teaspoons freshly ground black pepper

2 lemons, quartered

THIS IS A QUICK WAY TO COOK TROUT, at home over a charcoal fire or in the woods over a campfire. You will technically steam the trout inside the tightly secured foil, which will marry the juices from the fish with the vegetables.

Try to find spring onions (resembling giant scallions) in the market; they are worth seeking out because of their juicy sweetness. Vidalia or other sweet onions will suffice.

I was grilling freshly caught Atlantic salmon on the Matane River on Quebec's Gaspé Peninsula in this manner when two Provincial Conservation Officers drove up. They were curious about the smoke they saw coming from the edge of the river. When they spied the salmon, they stayed awhile, helping to pick away at the fish and chatting about the weather conditions—cold and rainy, but, of course, that meant good fishing.

Prepare a charcoal grill.

Heat the oil in a medium sauté pan over medium-high heat. Add the pumpkin seeds and toast, stirring constantly, for about 2 minutes. (Pumpkin seeds pop like popcorn so you will need to cover them or use a wire mesh guard over the top of the pan.) Transfer to paper towels and set aside.

Remove the head and tail from the trout, rinse, and pat dry. Butterfly them. Lay out four 12 x 18-inch pieces of aluminum foil and place one trout on each piece, skin side down. Place 2 tablespoons butter, 5 chives, 5 garlic chives, 1 piece onion, and 1 piece of tomato on top of each trout and sprinkle each with about 1 teaspoon cumin, ½ teaspoon salt, ½ teaspoon pepper, and 1 tablespoon of pumpkin seeds. Squeeze 1 lemon wedge over each trout and lay the wedge on top. Fold the ends of foil over the fish, bring sides up, and pinch all together tightly to form a secure seal.

When the charcoal is gray and hot, or a wood fire has burned down to coals, place the foil packets on the grate of the grill, skin side up. Grill for 5 minutes. Turn and grill for 3 minutes more.

Remove the packets from the grate and open the foil. With a spatula, transfer each piece of fish to a warm plate, drizzle any juices over it, and serve immediately, with extra lemon wedges.

To Drink

A Fumé Blanc from Grgich Hills, Napa Valley, a concentrated classic Sauvignon Blanc, intense with onion and herb flavors, is appropriate with this trout recipe and to be enjoyed in the great outdoors or at home on a patio.

Or, from France's Loire Valley, another Sauvignon Blanc, the Sancerre, Clos de Perrieres, is flinty, crisp, and refreshing.

Chopin, Trout, and the Sea

henever I think trout I hear Chopin. An unconscious thread exists on the stream and in my head. Delicate, powerful, hesitant, forceful, the smooth surface of a flowing creek shows little of its determination. Like a well-crafted piano sonata.

One cool May evening as a caddis hatch emerged from the Konkapot River, I was day-dreaming, recalling a favorite sonata and thinking about its correlation with stream fishing. The small river weaves and meanders through greening pastures, gurgling over century-old fallen millstones. A chickadee flits from branch to branch, and the occasional orange flash of an oriole darts across my vision, the only departure from an otherwise tranquil moment.

I seek late-day equilibrium, grasping for a sense of the timid, still hour. I proceed with a calculated rhythm, watching for any indication of a theme or its variation. Ripples appear, disappear. The startling rise of a driven fish; a frantic attack at my fly. A narrow miss, but a promise for another time. My mind drifts purposefully, like the current. A tranquil evening closes with glimpses of delicate, interwoven themes.

At home I case my rod, put on Chopin's piano sonata in B-flat minor, and sit down to close my eyes. The image of a quiet riffle on the Kinkapot meshes with flowing sound like the welcoming handshake of a dear friend.

The next day brings a report of striped bass running up the Massachusetts Cape Cod coast. I pack my gear and within a few hours am hooking up my waders on a Truro beach, exactly twenty-four hours after having set out for trout.

I could not help but contrast the activities: trout fishing in a gentle freshwater stream, forceful salt-water fishing. Here at the brink of the sea, waves thrash me, scooping sand from beneath my boots and making me stumble momentarily. I'm knocked backward. As I recompose myself and resume casting, symphonic strains begin to dance once again through my brain. But not a piano sonata. Different. Stronger. Bigger. The rising power of a crescendo propels my thoughts forward, out into the water.

I fight the driving wind and catch myself before I lean too far into a wave. Salt water sprays, stinging my eyes. A flock of sea ducks line the horizon, skimming inches over the surface of the water. The urgent flapping of wings sounds a staccato rhythm.

I walk the beach toward a jetty. The incoming tide carves a rip I cast beyond. I look down to clumps of sea grass sweeping past my boots, dragged in by the force of the tide and heading up the Palmet River. In a few short hours they will rush aimlessly back, seaward, hitchhiking the outgoing tide. Waves beat on jetty rocks like the boom of a timpani. My ears throb as I lurch back again, forced by the determined waves.

Flocks of seagulls chase swirling, splashing schools of frenzied bait-fish. Here, there, diving frantically for food, out into the fierce gusts, then back toward land. Perhaps they're following a striper in pursuit of some prey. Laser fast the cawing birds dip like the flash of a conductor's baton. Their repetitive squawks sound syncopated but when I listen carefully completely arrhythmic, meshing with the crashing of the waves.

Crazily now, I think I see it, a cathedral rising through the mist beyond my bright yellow fly. A Gothic buttress shoots skyward as French horns surge, and the structure becomes fixed in my mind before a purple haze sprays it over with disbelief. My shoulder strains as the streamlined striper fly retreats for the last time, skipping arrowlike through the tips of breaking waves. It is past sundown. The wind has picked up, and my glasses are flecked with sea-water. No matter. I can still see as I walk back along the darkened shore, staying inside the dunes to avoid the ocean's lancing spray.

Overhead, streaks of light intertwine, a horizontal aurora borealis monumentally off course. I hear a final Debussy refrain: deep-throated brass, a zippy chorus of strings, pounding timpani rolls pulse toward the climax of a cymbal crash—a holistic light show with Dolby sound.

My mind is a kaleidoscope, dazzled by the wind, the spray, the throbbing music, a bizarre, fantastic notion. Spent, I stroll back to the car. I don't recall packing away my gear.

When I get home, the CD on the player, where I left it, I flip a switch and sink into my red leather chair, thankful to be back near the soothing sonata of trout water.

Potato-Wrapped Salmon Kabobs

Serves 4

3-4 lemons

2 cups reduced-sodium soy sauce

8 tablespoons wasabi or Chinese yellow mustard powder

2 teaspoons sugar

24 1½-inch cubes of skinless salmon (approximately 3-4 pounds of fillets)

24 pearl onions, peeled

1 pound small white button mushrooms, cleaned but not stemmed

1 medium zucchini

1 large or 2 small red bell peppers, cored and seeded

1 large white potato, peeled

Vegetable oil for brushing

IN THIS DISH, the colorful salmon shows itself through the translucency of the thinly sliced potato. The delicate flavor of salmon is contrasted by the zingy, dipping sauce—made so by the bright addition of wasabi, the green horseradish powder that is possibly one of the few things that is able to make a Samurai warrior shed a tear.

Give your guests their own small mounds of freshly mixed wasabi to adjust the dipping sauce to their desired heat level and serve the kabobs with brown rice.

You will need a mandoline, a meat slicer, the slicing blade of a food processor, or a steady hand with a thin, sharp knife. If the potato slices are not thin enough they will snap in two. The slices are wrapped around each piece of salmon so if the potato is not large enough, you will need two slices of potato per piece of salmon. Slice extra pieces in case some do break.

Soak 24 12-inch-long wooden skewers and several wooden tooth picks in water for about 20 minutes, so they won't burn.

Squeeze 2 of the lemons. You should have 4-6 tablespoons of juice. Mix the soy sauce, 4 tablespoons wasabi powder, the sugar, and the lemon juice in a small bowl. Stir, pour half into another bowl, and reserve for later use. Add the salmon cubes to the first bowl of marinade. Cover and refrigerate.

Parboil the onions for 3-4 minutes, until just soft. Remove, drain, and let cool. Slice the mushrooms, zucchini, and bell pepper into 1½-inch x ¼-inch pieces, making sure you have 24 of each. Set aside.

Peel the potato and slice very, very thin. Immerse the potato slices in warm water so they don't turn brown and to soften them.

Light a charcoal fire.

Remove the salmon from the marinade, discarding the marinade. Wrap each piece of salmon with potato slices and secure with a toothpick. If you need to use two pieces of potato, secure them with one toothpick where they overlap.

Place the prepared ingredients on the skewers in this order: salmon—through the open end of the fish cube, not through the potato—then green squash, onion, bell pepper, and mushroom. Repeat to include three of everything on each skewer. Brush each skewer with oil.

When the charcoal is gray and hot lay the skewers on the grill, watching carefully so the potato does not burn. Raise the grate higher if this occurs. Grill 4-5 minutes, baste with more oil, turn, and grill another 4-5 minutes or until the salmon is cooked through.

Mix the remaining 4 tablespoons wasabi powder with 1-2 teaspoons of water (or as needed) and stir into a paste. Serve on the side with the reserved soy sauce marinade for dipping.

Remove the skewers and squeeze fresh lemon juice over the fish and vegetables before serving. Cut up any remaining lemon into wedges and serve on the side.

NOTE: Wasabi powder and Chinese yellow mustard powder are sold in the Asian products section of supermarkets.

Panfried Large-Mouth Bass

Serves 4

8 tablespoons butter (about ½ cup)

½ teaspoon canola oil

1-2 whole bass (or any freshwater white fish), about 3-4 pounds, headless

1 large white onion, thinly sliced

3 large potatoes, thinly sliced

1 teaspoon salt

2 teaspoons freshly ground black pepper

2-3 lemons, sliced

Nasturtium flowers, for garnish (optional)

Parsley, for garnish

To Drink

Try a Fumé Blanc from a reliable Napa Valley producer such as Grgich Hills. Grgich Hills make this classic Sauvignon Blanc with intensity and lots of herbal and fruit flavors. Or Springbok's Sauvignon Blanc from South Africa is a light, fruity and delicious white wine that pairs well with fish and onions.

ONE FALL EVENING JUST AFTER we had opened for dinner, four guests arrived at Konkapot Restaurant in Mill River, Massachusetts, on their way to hear the Boston Symphony Orchestra at Tanglewood. In front of the restaurant a friend was hoisting three huge large-mouth bass from his automobile. The guests watched as the fisherman marched through the front door of the restaurant, through the dining room, and into the kitchen. The waitress soon inquired of me if the "really fresh" fish was one of the evening's specials; I sent the prep person out to scale and clean the fish while I sliced potatoes and onions. A platter arrived at the concertgoers' table mounded with the freshest of ingredients (including lettuce, tomatoes, and onions direct from our garden). The guests later told me they had never before enjoyed such a fresh and spontaneous meal.

Melt the butter with the oil in a large cast-iron skillet over medium heat. Place the fish in the middle of the pan and surround it with the sliced onions and potatoes (you can briefly parboil the potatoes). Sprinkle with salt and pepper. Cover partially, leaving the lid slightly askew so the moisture escapes, and sauté for 15 minutes. Turn everything once and cook for another 15-30 minutes, until the fish turned white and the potatoes are cooked. Remove the cover about 10 minutes before the end of the cooking period.

Remove the backbone from the fish and reassemble it to appear whole before taking the platter to the table (see page 180).

Arrange the fish, potatoes, and onions on a warmed oval platter, garnish with nasturtium flowers and parsley, and serve with lemon wedges.

Sweet Potato, Walleye & Onion Pie

Serves 6

THE SWEET POTATOES ADD an extra hint of sweetness and color to this casserole. The onions impart their natural sweet flavoring to the dish as well. Cut the onions as you would onion rings.

Preheat the oven to 375°F.

Bring a large saucepan full of water to a boil and add the sweet potatoes. Cook for about 15 minutes, or until a fork easily pierces the potatoes. Drain, transfer to a large mixing bowl, and mash with half the melted butter until smooth. Set aside.

Brush the bottom and sides of a 14 x 10 x 2-inch ovenproof baking pan with some of the melted butter.

With a rubber spatula, cover the bottom of the pan with a 1-inch layer of sweet potatoes. Add a layer of half of the onions, half of the red peppers, half of the fish fillets, half of the lemon juice, half of the yogurt, 1 tablespoon Trinidad masala, ½ teaspoon salt, 1 teaspoon black pepper, and another layer of sweet potatoes. Repeat the layering to fill the pan. With a rubber spatula, top with the remaining sweet potatoes. Set aside.

In the bowl of a food processor combine the bread crumbs, cornmeal, cheese, basil, parsley, remaining black pepper, and remaining 1 teaspoon of Trinidad masala. Process for about 1 minute, or until thoroughly blended. Spoon the mixture over the top of the sweet potatoes and drizzle the remaining melted butter over the bread crumbs.

Cover with aluminum foil and bake for about 45 minutes. Remove the foil and bake 10-15 minutes more, until the crumbs are lightly browned.

Cut the pie into equal portions and serve on warm plates, with a separate salad.

---

4 medium sweet potatoes, peeled and cut into 1-inch chunks (about 7 cups)

¾ cup melted butter

4 large sweet white onions, cut into ⅛-inch slices (about 4 cups)

2 roasted red bell peppers, cut into 1-inch strips

2 walleye, northern pike, bass, or any other white fish fillets, cut into 1-inch strips

Juice of 1 lemon

2 cups plain low-fat yogurt

2 tablespoons plus 1 teaspoon Trinidad masala (see mail-order sources) or curry powder

1 teaspoon salt

3 teaspoons freshly ground black pepper

1 cup bread crumbs

¼ cup cornmeal

¾ cup grated Parmesan cheese

1 tablespoon finely chopped fresh basil

1 tablespoon finely chopped fresh parsley

Striped Bass with Snow Peas, Shiitake Mushrooms & Rice Noodles

Serves 4

I'VE ENJOYED STRIPED BASS since the early days of the Martha's Vineyard Striped Bass and Bluefish Derbies. But I recall the colder fall days of late October and November, after the derby, as being the best time for stripers; the best fishing was after midnight.

Fortunately, the tide has turned for the return of sport fishing for stripers. Their numbers are on the increase today.

Bring 3 quarts of water to a boil in a large pot. Place a colander or strainer over the top, place the fish inside, cover, and steam for 8-10 minutes, until the fish is firm and white. Remove the colander, let the fish cool, and flake into small pieces, discarding the bones. Set aside.

Lower the rice noodles into the boiling water. Boil for 3 minutes and transfer to a colander. Run hot water over the noodles and toss with 1 tablespoon of the canola oil to keep them from sticking together. Set aside. (The very thin variety of noodles requires only a warm soaking for 20 minutes instead.)

Heat the sesame oil and the remaining ½ tablespoon canola oil in a wok over high heat. Add the sesame seeds and toast for about 1 minute. Add the snow peas and shiitakes. Toss with the sesame mixture. Sauté for 3-4 minutes. Add the rice wine, fish sauce, and pepper. Stir and sauté about 2 minutes. Add the fish pieces and noodles and toss together for about 1 minute, making sure the noodles and vegetables combine thoroughly.

Transfer to warm plates and squeeze fresh lemon juice over each serving. Serve with additional lemon wedges.

8 ounces striped bass

4 ounces rice noodles

1½ tablespoons canola or vegetable oil

1 tablespoon Asian sesame oil

2 tablespoons sesame seeds

2 cups snow peas, cut into thirds

1 cup diced fresh shiitake mushrooms

2 tablespoons rice wine

2 tablespoons Thai fish sauce (nam pla)

1 teaspoon freshly ground black pepper

1 lemon, cut into wedges

To Drink

A slightly peppery Rioja from Spain pairs nicely with Asian foods. The Bodegas Berberana's Rioja Gran Reserva is a particularly decent wine, well developed with lots of cherry and coffee flavors. (The 85 was terrific.)

Baked Bluefish with Horseradish Mayonnaise

Serves 4 to 6

2 tablespoons lemon juice

2 teaspoons white vinegar

2 egg yolks

2 tablespoons fresh horseradish

1 teaspoon smooth Dijon mustard

Salt

½ cup olive oil

Zest of 1 lemon

1 4-5 pound bluefish, cleaned

2 small tomatoes, diced

4-5 scallions, thinly sliced (use most of green tops)

Black pepper

A GOOD RULE of thumb for cooking fish is 10 minutes per inch when measured at the thickest part of the fish. If your bluefish is much larger than the one recommended below, adjust the baking time.

Bake, grill, or broil any other fish with this mayonnaise. I also love to swirl a couple of tablespoons into Fish, Corn & Apple Chowder (see page 65) while heating. It's superb.

The mayonnaise can be made up to several days ahead and refrigerated.

To make the mayonnaise, blend the lemon juice, vinegar, egg yolks, horseradish, mustard, and ½ teaspoon salt in the bowl of a food processor. Pulse for 10-15 seconds and scrape down the sides with a rubber spatula.

Turn on the machine and drizzle the oil in very slowly through the feed tube until the liquids are emulsified, about 2-3 minutes. Do not rush or the mayonnaise will break. If it does, add a few drops of warm water, up to a teaspoon, and reprocess. Add the lemon zest, pulse 3-4 times until incorporated, transfer from bowl to a small container, and set aside. (Mayonnaise can be prepared ahead and refrigerated, covered.)

Lay the bluefish in a baking pan large enough to accommodate it. With a rubber spatula or a basting brush, smear mayonnaise inside the cavity and on both sides of the fish. Sprinkle tomatoes and scallions inside the cavity, around, and over the fish. Add additional salt and pepper if desired. Cover with aluminum foil and bake for 40-50 minutes, until cooked through.

Cut fish into steaks (or debone; see page 180), ladle any sauce from the pan over the fish, and garnish with extra lemon wedges and fresh dill.

Panfried Shad Roe

Serves 2

LIVING ALONG THE HUDSON RIVER in New York State for seven years, I was able to fish for feisty shad each spring and also to indulge in the fish's wonderful roe, which is exceptionally rich and high in cholesterol.

Old-timers like their roe cooked with bacon (which is like adding fat to the fire). If you have an old-timer around, substitute two slices of bacon for the butter and serve the roe with the bacon lying across the top. Frankly, I think freshly squeezed lemon juice and dill are the only added ingredients one needs.

Shad roe freezes well, losing little of its flavor or quality. If you love roe, stock up in the spring when it is fresh (see page 19).

If you like soft-shell crabs, follow this same recipe using the crabs in place of roe. It is a simple way to retain both of these delicacies' natural flavors.

4 tablespoons butter

½ teaspoon canola oil

¼ cup dry white wine

2 pair medium shad roe

2 tablespoons stemmed and finely chopped fresh dill

1 lemon, cut into wedges

Melt the butter with the oil in a large skillet over medium-high heat and pour in the wine. When the wine comes to a boil, in about 1 minute, gently place the roe in the pan (the egg sacks tear easily). Cover, turn down the heat to medium-low, and simmer 8-10 minutes. Turn once, gently, and cook uncovered for another 8-10 minutes, until the center of the roe is pink, like a medium-rare steak. (Some people prefer their roe cooked thoroughly.)

Sprinkle with fresh dill, squeeze lemon juice over the roe, and serve with extra lemon wedges on the side.

To Drink

From the Monterey region of California, Lockwood's Pinot Blanc has medium body, texture, and spicy components that would blend nicely with the simple richness of this meal.

Or Falconer Vineyard of California makes a full-bodied Russian River Valley Blanc de Blanc, Brut, a sparkling wine that is dry and tastes just fine in the spring with shad or shad roe.

Baked Shad with Toasted Sunflower Seeds

Serves 4

2 teaspoons canola oil

½ cup shelled unsalted sunflower seeds

2 tablespoons butter

4 garlic cloves, finely chopped

Juice of 1 lemon (2-3 tablespoons)

1 3-4 pound whole shad, cleaned

1 teaspoon salt

1 tablespoon black pepper

3-4 wild leeks (ramps) or 1 small leek thinly sliced and well cleaned, white part only

2 tablespoons dry white wine or water

8 large sorrel leaves

AMERICAN SHAD ARE THE LARGEST of the herring family and are an important commercial and sport fish along the Atlantic coast, valued for their meat as well as their roe.

Shad are anadromous—they spend most of their life in the ocean and return to fresh water to spawn. They run up the Hudson River from late April to early June. The Connecticut River has a similar run.

Shad have a migratory range of thousands of miles. In late spring shad head north to spend the summer in the Bay of Fundy. In the fall they head south to winter off the coasts of North Carolina and Virginia. Fishermen addicted to their ferocity often follow the migration up and down the East Coast.

No one likes fish bones. Shad, perhaps more than most fish, has them. Lots of bones. At New York's Fulton Fish Market, shad boning is undertaken by the few who know the technique. It requires years of experience to perfect the art, requiring some thirteen slices of the knife to eliminate all the bones.

But by baking the fish for a very long time at a low temperature, the bones become soft—nearly dissolved—and are edible; there is no need to bone the fish.

The arrival of migrating shad in the spring is often accompanied with the first harvest of sorrel, a fine accompaniment to shad.

Springtime should also see fresh fiddleheads start to sprout beside most rivers—on the bank and in sandy areas where there is some shade. Look for smooth-skinned fiddleheads. If you are not able to fetch your own, many markets now sell them.

Serve strawberry-rhubarb pie for dessert to round out the spring harvest.

P reheat the oven to 250°F.

Heat 1 teaspoon of the oil in a small sauté pan over medium heat and toast the sunflower seeds for about 1 minute, stirring constantly. Be watchful, they burn quickly. Transfer the nuts to paper towels with a slotted spoon to blot and set aside.

Combine the butter, garlic, and half of the lemon juice, and rub the shad inside and out with the mixture. Add salt and pepper. Place half of the sunflower seeds and half of the leeks inside the cavity of the fish.

Brush the remaining 1 teaspoon of canola oil on the shiny side of a piece of heavy-duty aluminum foil that will accommodate the fish with an extra 6 inches on all sides. Lay the fish on the foil and bring up all four sides to create a basinlike container. Sprinkle on the remaining sunflower seeds and leeks, pour the remainder of the lemon juice over the fish, and add the wine to the foil. Crimp the foil together, forming a tight seal. Lay in a large baking pan and place into the oven for 5 hours.

Just before serving, blanch the sorrel leaves in boiling water for about 30 seconds. Remove and pat dry on paper towels. Remove the fish from the oven, unwrap, and divide into 4 servings. Place each portion over 2 leaves of fresh sorrel, pour any juices over the fish, and serve with lemon wedges on the side.

To Drink

Castello d'Albola produces a crispy and light Pinot Grigio, a fine complement to the leeks and sorrel.

Or a dry Côtes de Provence Rosé, such as the one from Château La Moutete, also has the subtlety and fruit to blend with the delicate white flesh of shad.

Fly Fisherman's Fancy

I grew up, like most boys, fishing with worms. A fly was something you swatted.

The "fly" in fly-fishing is often an imitation of an aquatic insect, some nearly indistinguishable from the real thing, others no larger than the head of a pin. Many who tie their own flies do so for economic reasons; commercially tied flies can be expensive, considering you can lose several in a day's outing. There are fishermen who tie flies as an end in itself. A skillfully tied salmon fly, for example, is often widely appreciated for its artful design and array of multicolored feathers. Some become collector's items. I have a beauty, framed and sitting on my desk.

Fly-fishing is a genteel sport, requiring patience. It affords the sportsman countless hours of solitude, time to ponder the words of, say, Henry David Thoreau or Theodore Gordon, the founding father of American fly-fishing.

Fly-fishermen tend to resemble the ectomorphic sort Robert Redford immortalized in his 1992 movie of Norman MacLean's novel, *A River Runs Through It*: gaunt, sinewy, single-malt-scotch-sipping, literary, clenched-teeth individuals who probably possess smoking jackets and advanced degrees. But we're not all bad. We're simply hooked.

There is something deeper, intrinsic to our nature, though. We have a major weakness: we can be spotted a mile off. Plumage, dress-up, self-adornment—that is what we do best, well, next to tying teeny little chicken feathers onto smaller-still hooks. Yes sir, we do dress the part.

Most fly-fishers orchestrate garbs fit for a king or queen. Paris spring fashions have nothing over the latest in angling wear for day and night, all piscatorially embroidered and embellished. Long, cold winter nights pass quickly when spent perusing one of the now hundreds of catalogs aimed at the boutique-minded outdoors-person's wallet.

Let's start at the top, where a fisherman has countless hats to choose: a Moose River hat, the Stetson Open Road, felt crusher hats, waxed cottons, cowboy hats (for western waters), touring caps, suede sports caps (with or without advertising), boat hats, straw sun helmets, archer's hats, and, in alphabetical order by country: African safari hats, Australian bush hats, English kangol caps, Greek fisherman's hats, Gurkha Regiment hats, Irish tweed hats, Macora South American plantation hats, and one of my favorites—the Panama straw hat.

Moving on down to the upper torso we come to that signature piece of clothing, the vest, now being copied for the general market by Ralph Lauren, Bill Blass, and any other fashion designer worth their bolts. But theirs is not the same as ours. Ours have more utilitarian pockets, plus that fuzzy little lamb's wool fly-drying patch stuck high up on the chest. Ours are pragmatic; no frills here.

A typical well-designed vest supports thirty-six (count 'em) pockets in which to stash several fly boxes jammed with flies of every size, color, and pattern, for any stream, river, ocean, season, state, province, beat, or country; several spools of leader material; a spare reel in case one needs to switch lines from stream to stream; scissors to cut line; a hook remover; a barometer; a magnifying glass attachment for eyeglasses that let you see the unbelievably small dry flies and microcosmically thin line; a thermometer to tell water temperature (no sense being out there if the fish are smart enough to stay home); fly-dope, the kind intended to keep real flies away; a compact camera with which to record the fish, since catch-and-release has become the unspoken standard; a scale, in order to maintain probity; a palm-size camcorder (for the braggart in most of us); a tape recorder to document stream conditions and the hatch for next year's reference; spare polarized glasses, for day fishing; a coal miner's headlamp, for night fishing; an engraved silver flask, also for night fishing; a Swiss army knife, the big one with the fold-out fly-tiers table and vise; spare rain gear; a collapsible wading staff; pipe and tobacco paraphernalia; a portable GPS tracking system that shows lost fishermen where to go, and how to get there, on the newest graphical satellite status LED screen; a fisherman's watch, the one with a daily moon phase chart and sunrise and sunset tables; a United States quarter and an English pound (or—how could I forget, these days, a cell phone), in case you need to telephone in an emergency; perhaps an antique sandwich in the back pouch from the previous trip; and a battery-operated miniature food processor to assist with an appropriate lunch for a health-conscious yuppie away from home. It gets tough

to breath with all that stuff hanging from your chest.

The $125 Hemingway Bush poplin shirt underneath sports about as many pockets. But these good-looking shirts are more likely filled with personal items: a Ducks Unlimited monogrammed fourteen-carat gold pen, credit

cards, waterproof topo maps, sunscreen, extra film, a nine-volt battery-operated weather radio, a collapsible metal detector for finding lost hooks, and of course, I.D., so if the damn fool falls in the river and drowns the hospital knows where to ship the body.

From the back of a well-dressed fisher swings a beautiful handmade bent-ash and bird's-eye maple net, banging between the thirteenth and fourteenth vertebrae. The designer net serves a twofold purpose: first, to net fish; and second—with only a little awkwardness, the net will hold one 750 milliliter bottle of California chardonnay, which, hung low enough, gets conveniently chilled by lunchtime. An old Theodore Gordon technique, I've heard.

Descending lower still, we come to those ugly-green or dismal-brown waders. They are extremely unsightly, even the camouflage ones that allegedly can't be seen. Any sleek-looking fisherman who spends his lunch hours working out in a gym wants to show off his physique—impossible in the older rubber waders, barely possible with neoprenes.

Booties and gaiters—well, fortunately Paris hasn't discovered those. They remain purely functional, camouflage or dull brown in color and waterproof. No chiffon, gold lamé, or silver tinsel. Yet.

I think it appropriate to offer another angler's viewpoint on this contemporary propensity toward self-adornment. After all, I wouldn't like members of the fly-fishing community taking offense at these observations to believe I am alone in my opinions. So, here is an excerpt from *The Angler*, a book of essays by the Catskill angler and author Washington Irving, that is as apt today as when he wrote it, fresh from a stay in England, where he was tutored in "the gentle art" of fly fishing. Irving had been in the company of several American friends and had studied Isaac Walton's *Compleat Angler*, the fisherman's bible:

It was early in the year, but as soon as the weather was auspicious and that the spring began to melt into the verge of summer, we took rod in hand and sallied into the country, as stark mad as was even Don Quixote.

One of our party had equalled the Don in the fullness of his equipments, being attired a cap-a-pie for the enterprise. He wore a broad-skirted fustian coat perplexed with half a hundred pockets, a pair of stout shoes and leathern gaiters, a basket slung on one side for fish, a patent rod, a landing net, and a score of other inconveniences only to be found in the true anglers armory. Thus harnessed for the field, he was as great a matter of stare and wonderment among the country folk, who had never seen a regular angler, as was the steel-clad hero of La Mancha . . .

Washington Irving published this essay in 1819, thirty-seven years before Charley Orvis put out his first catalog and almost a century before Leon L. Bean started hawking his boots up there in Maine.

Grilled Northern Pike
with Cucumbers & Pine Nuts

Serves 4

PIKE IS AN UNDERRATED freshwater fish. I'm sure it gets its bad rap from the number of small bones it harbors. It is one of the sweetest white fish I know and if one is willing to cope with the bones, the final results are well worth the effort. Its cousins, the smaller pickerel and the giant muskellunge, fall into the same cursed category of bony fish.

The marriage of fish with sweet, white cucumbers has a long history. This preparation combines the cucumbers with the delicate nuttiness of pine nuts to enhance the overall sweetness of pike.

Light a charcoal fire.

Heat the oil in a medium skillet over medium-low heat. Add the pine nuts when the oil is hot, stirring constantly until golden brown, about 1 minute. Be watchful; they tend to burn very quickly. Transfer the pine nuts to paper towels and set aside.

Melt the butter in the same skillet and add the cucumber. Sauté over low heat for 10-15 minutes, until translucent. Add the scallions and sauté for another 2 minutes. Remove from the heat, stir in the pine nuts, and keep warm.

When the charcoal is gray and hot, lay the fish fillets on the grate. Grill 6-8 minutes on each side, until the fish is tender, flaky, and translucent. (An old Canadian rule of thumb: cook fish 10 minutes per inch when fish is measured at its thickest part.)

Season the fish with salt and pepper. Serve with the cucumber mixture ladled over the fish. Just before serving, squeeze fresh lemon juice over the fish, with extra wedges on the side, and season with salt and pepper.

1 teaspoon canola oil

6 tablespoons pine nuts

2 tablespoons butter

1 cucumber, peeled, seeded, and thinly sliced

6 small scallions, trimmed and sliced on the diagonal

1 3-4 pound fillet of pike, pickerel, muskellunge, or freshwater bass

1 teaspoon salt

1 tablespoon freshly ground black pepper

1-2 lemons, cut into wedges

To Drink

Try a sparkling Carneros wine from California: Brut Carneros Royal Cuvée by Gloria Ferrer, a dazzling champagnelike wine with cherry and vanilla flavors, ripe and complex.

Santa Barbara's Au Bon Climat's Il Podere Tocai Friulano is lively and finishes nicely with a crisp, refreshing tang.

Grilled Swordfish with Blood Orange Mayonnaise

Serves 4

1 large egg

1 egg yolk

1 tablespoon Dijon mustard

2 tablespoons fresh lemon juice

2 teaspoons white vinegar

1 teaspoon Triple Sec or any other orange-flavored liqueur

1 teaspoon salt

¼ cup blood orange juice (or other freshly squeezed orange juice), about ½ orange

½ cup olive oil

Zest of ½ orange

2 pounds swordfish, about 1½ inches thick

1 lemon, cut into wedges

WHEN I LIVED AND WORKED on Martha's Vineyard, I befriended a swordfisherman who invited me to a big barbecue. My friend showed me how he prepared fish for his crew: swab down the steaks with mayonnaise (he used a commercial brand) and grill them.

Blood oranges are available in the early spring. You can substitute any sweet orange, but the color won't be as brilliant.

Start a charcoal fire.

To make the mayonnaise, blend the egg, egg yolk, mustard, lemon juice, vinegar, Triple Sec, salt, and orange juice in a food processor. Pulse for 10-15 seconds and scrape down the sides with a rubber spatula.

Turn on the machine and drizzle the oil in very slowly through the feed tube until the liquids are emulsified, about 2-3 minutes. Do not rush or the mayonnaise may break. If it does, add a few drops of warm water, up to a teaspoon, and reprocess.

Add the orange zest, pulse 3-4 times until incorporated, then transfer to a small container, cover, and refrigerate. (The recipe can be prepared ahead up to this point.)

A few hours before grilling, brush a liberal amount of the mayonnaise on both sides of the fish and return it to the refrigerator. Remove the fish from the refrigerator 15 minutes before grilling.

When the coals are gray and hot, lay the fish on the grate. Grill 5-6 minutes on each side, until lightly charred on the outside, leaving the inside slightly rare. If you do not like fish cooked rare, add 1-2 minutes per side.

Remove the fish and serve with additional mayonnaise on the side, along with an ample supply of lemon wedges.

Fish Stew

1 cup mayonnaise

2 teaspoons finely chopped garlic

1 pound fish heads and frames

2 large potatoes, scrubbed and diced

1 medium onion, coarsely chopped

1 stalk celery, finely chopped

2 carrots, finely chopped

¼ cup stemmed fresh dill

¼ cup stemmed fresh parsley

1 teaspoon chopped fresh tarragon

1 teaspoon salt (or to taste)

1 teaspoon ground black pepper

1 cup dry white wine

2 pounds white nonoily fish fillets, such as bass, pike, or walleye, cut into 8 pieces

1 large tomato, seeded and diced

¼ cup Pernod or Ricard

12 mussels, scrubbed and debearded

8 shelled shrimp

8 scallops

1 fresh baguette, in ½-inch slices

Fresh parsley, for garnish

Chopped red bell pepper, for garnish

THERE ARE PROBABLY as many fish stew recipes as there are fishermen and cooks, and no two are ever alike. Whatever the theory, an aromatic, richly flavored fish stew has no equal.

Personally, I find it difficult to eat a fish stew without lots of garlic mayonnaise and crusty French bread.

Combine the mayonnaise and garlic in a small bowl. Whisk together, cover, and refrigerate.

Wrap the fish heads and frames in a 24 x 24-inch piece of cheesecloth and tie tightly. In a large saucepan or stockpot over medium heat combine the fish heads and frames, potatoes, onion, celery, carrots, dill, parsley, tarragon, salt, and pepper. Add 4 cups of water and ½ cup of wine. Bring to a boil, then reduce heat to low. Cover and simmer for 45 minutes.

In another large pot, add the fish fillets, tomato, and 1 cup of water. Cover, bring to a boil, and reduce the heat to low. Simmer for 6-8 minutes, until fish has turned white. Add the remaining ½ cup wine, Pernod, mussels, shrimp, and scallops. Bring to a boil, reduce heat to low, and simmer for 5 minutes.

Remove the cheesecloth containing fish heads and frames from the stockpot. Squeeze out as much liquid as you can back into the pot and discard the bag.

Swirl 1 tablespoon of garlic mayonnaise in the bottom of each of 4 serving bowls. Smear garlic mayonnaise on baguette pieces and set aside.

With a slotted spoon remove the fish fillets from their pot and divide among the bowls. Divide the scallops, mussels, and shrimp among the bowls. Ladle in some liquid from the pot and some of the stock, potatoes, and vegetables until each bowl is filled. Float 3-4 baguette pieces on the surface of each stew and serve immediately.

Garnish with fresh parsley and chopped red pepper.

Fish, Corn & Apple Chowder

IF IT IS HEARTY ENOUGH and has lots of fresh fish and vegetables, I find chowder to be filling enough to serve as a main course for dinner. Don't forget the oyster crackers.

Bring 2 quarts of water to a boil in a small saucepan and add the salt pork. Blanch over medium heat for 8 minutes to remove excess salt. Drain, cool, and dice into ¼-inch cubes.

Heat the oil over medium-high heat in a large saucepan or stockpot. Add the salt pork and fry for 10-12 minutes or until browned and crispy. Drain, reserving fat. Return 2 tablespoons of fat to the pot and set the drained salt pork aside. Discard excess fat.

Add the onion, celery, and apples, and sauté for 10-12 minutes, until the ingredients are thoroughly cooked. Add the fish stock and potatoes, and simmer over medium heat for about 15 minutes.

In a small saucepan over medium heat bring milk and cream nearly to a boil and remove from the heat. Add to the large saucepan containing vegetables and stock. Add the corn, fish, browned salt pork, Old Bay Seasoning, salt, and pepper. Stir and simmer over low heat, never boiling, for about 15 minutes, covered. Add the chives, remove from the heat, and ladle into soup bowls. (Strain and remove salt pork pieces if desired.) Serve immediately, garnished with finely chopped red bell pepper.

8 ounces salt pork, skin removed

1 tablespoon canola or corn oil

1 medium sweet white onion, finely chopped (about 1 cup)

2 stalks celery, finely chopped (about ¾ cup)

2 apples, peeled, cored, and diced (about 1 cup)

2 cups fish stock

2 medium potatoes, peeled and diced

2 cups milk

1 cup heavy cream

2½ cups fresh corn kernels

1 pound firm white fish fillets such as bass, pike, striped bass, or cod, flaked or cut into 1-inch cubes

3 tablespoons Old Bay Seasoning or paprika

½ teaspoon salt (or to taste)

1 teaspoon freshly ground black pepper

1 tablespoon finely chopped chives or scallions

2-3 tablespoons finely chopped red bell pepper, for garnish

Ducks, Pheasants, Quail, Grouse

& Other Game Birds

Smoked Hoisin Duck Legs over Couscous

Serves 4

1 cup hoisin sauce

½ cup dry sherry

4 tablespoons lemon juice

1 tablespoon freshly ground black pepper

8 meaty mallard or other large duck legs with thighs

1¾ cups low-sodium chicken stock

1 pound couscous

To Drink:

The Cabernet Sauvignon Coonawarra from the reliable Australian vintner Rosemount is dense, yet smooth, with much currant and cherry flavor. I like many of Rosemount's reds, but this is a particularly fine Cabernet. I still have some of the 1992 left, but not for long.

Or, a soft and round Merlot from Spain's Vega Sindoa is delicious, also with the currant and cherry flavors that go so well with duck.

WE INTRODUCED THIS RECIPE in the first year of Konkapot Restaurant, when I spent a lot of time smoking foods. (A close friend once told me he thought the only thing I hadn't smoked was broccoli.) I smoked hams, Canadian bacon, salmon, shrimp, lobster, cheeses, and turkeys—among other things—and many, many ducks.

This dish goes nicely with sautéed snap peas in butter, with toasted sesame seeds and a squeeze of fresh lemon.

Mix the hoisin sauce, sherry, lemon juice, and pepper in a large mixing bowl. Make several small slits in the skin and flesh of the duck legs and thighs. Inject the solution into the meat with a meat syringe and/or immerse the legs in the marinade overnight, refrigerated.

The next day, light a charcoal fire in a backyard smoker. (See page 180.)

When the charcoal is gray and hot, remove the duck legs from the marinade and lay them on the top grate of the smoker. Cover and smoke for about 2½-3 hours, until the meat is firm when touched. Turn about halfway through and baste with the marinade. Replenish charcoal and wood chips as needed.

To make the couscous, place the stock in a large saucepan with a colander suspended over the top. Add any duck giblets and parts to the stock for added intensity. Place the couscous in the colander lined with a clean towel, cover with a clean cloth or aluminum foil and bring stock to a boil. Steam for about 30 minutes (or 5 minutes if using the quick-cooking variety), stirring often with a wooden spoon. It should be light and fluffy.

Remove the duck legs from the smoker and brush with warmed marinade before serving. Serve 2 legs per person over a bed of the couscous.

NOTE: Hoisin sauce is available in the Asian foods section of supermarkets.

Breast of Mallard with Morels & Pistachio-Encrusted Figs

Serves 4

THE COOKING TIME RECOMMENDED here for duck breasts is for medium-rare. You can increase or reduce the time depending upon your preference. Many old-timers prefer their wild duck meat blood-rare.

Serve with wild rice and a spinach salad with orange slices, apples, and black olives.

Soak the dried morels in sherry for about 30 minutes.

Crush the pistachios with a mortar and pestle or grind in a small, clean coffee grinder until finely pulverized. Cut the figs into halves and flatten. With your thumb or the back of a spoon, firmly press the pistachios into the meaty part of the figs.

Heat the butter in a heavy, large skillet over medium-low heat and gently add the figs. Sauté the encrusted figs for only about 30 seconds on both sides, until the nuts are browned. Remove quickly and set aside.

In the same pan, heat the oil over medium-high heat. Sauté the duck breasts for 6-8 minutes, uncovered, until browned. Turn the duck breasts over and add the morels with the sherry, the brandy, and the stock. Simmer for 6-8 minutes, until thoroughly cooked. Turn off the heat, remove the pan from the stove, and set the figs into the pan to warm.

Transfer the breasts to a wooden platter and slice thinly. Fan about half a breast per person over a mound of wild rice and divide the morels and figs equally among the 4 plates. Scrape any remaining browned bits and juices from the pan onto the meat.

¼ ounce dried morel mushrooms

½ cup dry sherry

¼ cup shelled pistachios

4 fresh figs

2 tablespoons butter

1 tablespoon olive oil

2 mallard breasts, cleaned and trimmed of any fat or membrane (or substitute any large, meaty duck breasts)

¼ cup brandy (optional)

¼ cup chicken stock (or 2 bouillon cubes dissolved in ¼ cup water)

Duck Confit

Serves 4 to 6

3-4 wild ducks or 2 domestic ducks
  (about 8-9 pounds)

2 cups coarse (kosher) salt

6-8 pounds lard

½ head garlic cloves, peeled

MAKING CONFIT IS A LONG PROCESS, and one needs to plan ahead. Traditionally, confit (duck or goose slow cooked and preserved in fat) should be made weeks or months ahead. If necessary, it can be used immediately, but the aging process is what makes this dish, with its softened, buttery texture, special.

If you want good confit, you must cook it for a long time at a low temperature. The good news is that it will keep for a very long time packed away in duck or goose fat—or lard, as I use here.

You can get lard from your butcher, or look for 1-pound blocks in the meat department of most supermarkets.

You can confit the necks and wings to serve as an appetizer for another meal.

Clean and quarter the ducks, separating the legs and thighs. Reserve the giblets for stock or another use. Set aside the necks. Trim off all excess fat and leave most of the skin intact. Bone the breasts if you wish (they will take up less space during cooking). Cut off the wings and set aside.

Mix the duck pieces, including necks and wings, and salt in a large mixing bowl. Toss thoroughly, cover, and refrigerate overnight.

The next day, wash the duck pieces in cold water and pat dry. Set aside.

Heat 6 pounds of lard (or a mixture of lard with duck or goose fat) in a heavy, large pot over medium heat. Slowly melt the fat until the temperature reaches 190°F. Maintaining the 190° temperature, place the garlic cloves and duck pieces in the fat, making sure they are completely submerged.

The temperature will drop when the cold duck is added so you will need to turn up the heat slightly. Bring it back slowly to 190°F. and then reduce to low. Maintain this temperature for about 2 hours, never allowing it to vary. Then shut off the heat and let the duck pieces cool down completely covered by the fat for 20-30 minutes, until cool.

Remove the duck pieces, drain, and set aside. Once the fat has cooled a bit (do not let it cool completely or it will solidify), strain it through 2 layers of cheesecloth. Place the duck pieces in the bottom of a wide-mouthed clay crock or glass jar, separating the necks and wings from the breast and legs. Cover completely with the clean fat. Melt and add more if needed. Cover and refrigerate.

The next day, check the crock. The pieces will have settled and some air pockets may appear. Fill the spaces with more melted lard (not too hot) if necessary. Keep in a cool place such as a root cellar or refrigerator to age until needed, but at least 2 months. Do not let the crock sit in temperatures over 40-45°F. or the duck may spoil.

To use, set the crock in a container of warm water until the fat has softened. Remove pieces of duck from the crock and wipe off the excess fat. Leave any unused portions completely covered by the fat. Cover with more fat and keep cool. It will keep for up to 6 months in the refrigerator.

Heat the duck pieces in a sauté pan over medium heat until warm or add to Cassoulet (see page 156).

A Hunting Companion

very hunter should have a companion, sometimes. I have a few good friends with whom I can savor the golden beauty of the morning sun flickering through juniper branches and the like, but generally I am a solo hunter. That means I leave when I'm ready and hunt where and for as long as I wish, or just lie back and take a nap. In the company of fellow hunters, however, I have spent twenty-two bleary-eyed hours driving to Ontario from Massachusetts, stopping only for gas and a quick bite. In years when I had a say in the matter, I elected to stay overnight in a motel. Now that is the more likely plan, to the chagrin of one sportsman in particular.

Having fished the Margaree River in Nova Scotia for several years now, Craig, that same friend, has calculated that if he packs up and leaves camp at 3:00 A.M. he will arrive home at precisely 5:00 P.M. that same day. (Why that's important I don't know.) He plans his trips methodically, however exhausting the drive. Not me anymore—I take my own vehicle these days and approach automobile travel in a more leisurely manner. For example, I like traveling through the state of Maine; I can sidetrack over to L.L. Bean in Freeport and quickly lower my credit card limit. If I feel like stopping at a restaurant I will, instead of trying to balance a sandwich on my lap while driving—no sense wasting time, Craig insists.

With my own vehicle, I can even—horrors—take an afternoon off for sight-seeing. It was the second or third trip to Cape Breton Island when my dedicated fishing buddy finally stopped fishing for one day and drove the mountainous Cabot Trail, an eight-hour auto tour as spectacular as the Isle of Sky in western Scotland. My buddy might even have admitted he liked it; I don't recall.

But I have a hunting companion with whom I'll go out of my way to spend time. A book conservator by trade—"Jeff Rigby, Library and Archive Conservation," his card reads—Jeff restores and preserves words and history for large museums as well as small collections. He is easy to be with, was president of the Latin club in his high school, loves opera, hosted a Super Bowl party last year, and grew up in Ohio, where he learned to hunt ducks. He is bespectacled, reserved, and usually soft-spoken, until a flock of ducks comes into view over the horizon. Jeff's feathers ruffle at the thought of descending ducks, let alone the sight.

One year we began a tradition I came to anticipate eagerly. For six weeks in November and December we met late Wednesday afternoons at a landing dock on the Hudson River in upstate New York. We'd load his canoe and our gear for an evening of duck hunting in the marshes and swampy estuaries along the river, paralleling Amtrak's route. Secluded areas on the inside of the railroad embankment are a favored habitat for waterfowl.

We used Jeff's small electric trolling motor on his canoe until it developed a mechanical problem, then had to paddle our way several evenings out into the mighty Hudson. That's not too tough, unless you happen to be bursting out of multiple layers of underwear, sweaters, heavy wool pants, a down parka, and a bulbous life jacket giving a fair approximation of the Pillsbury Dough Boy.

Getting to and from a blind could be eventful. One day we nearly passed a plastic garbage bag resting on a grassy hummock, when Jeff's environmentally caring nature clicked into gear. We agreed we should rid the scape of the eyesore and paddled over to the bag. It had been punctured slightly and was filled with foul-smelling water. Jeff was unable to lift the bag over the gunnel, it was so heavy, so he tethered it behind the canoe and we towed it the half-mile back to the landing, very slowly and across the bottom for the last 100 yards. Of course, it broke open. But only after we lifted it out of the water onto the cement landing. It was vile and disgusting, but since it was dark outside, we couldn't see what mysterious artifacts we'd adopted. I wondered, for a fleeting, gagging moment, what the slimy glob was that I was transferring into the plastic bag Jeff had brought down from his car. The fine leather gloves I wore had to be laundered the next day (I probably should have burned them); they rode home in the trunk.

We shot some ducks in those six weeks, but more than that we spent time together, occasionally hunkering behind tall reeds on shore and once talking so much we missed a duck that landed not twenty yards away. Jeff dubbed it "the duck with a sense of humor" as it flew off squawking at us, two inattentive hunters.

The first two Wednesdays were sunny, bright, and almost too beautiful for hunting. The changing purple-pink sunsets and swirling gray cloud formations dazzled us, hovering over the snow-capped Catskill Mountains across the water. If we had wanted nothing more than to enjoy the dramatic beauty, it was there for our pleasure as it had been for Frederic Church and Thomas Cole, two prominent artists of the renowned nineteenth-century Hudson River School of Painting. We were just two miles upriver from Church's house, Olana, now a museum. We were also a mere half-hour's drive from awe-inspiring Katterskill Falls, where you can still trace with your finger dozens of hundred-year-old names and dates, etched by Hudson River school painters with calligraphic flair into giant stones wedged into the riverbed. I could almost feel the creative vibes sizzling across the river.

On our third outing it snowed like a midwestern plains blizzard—horizontally and with driven fury. I had to turn my face away from the blinding flakes, they were so piercing. Jeff forgot his waterproof outerwear and got soaked to the skin, numbed.

Another evening we rounded a bend in one of the riverlike channels that flows through this swampy tidal backwater and scared up what we first thought were snow geese—somewhat unusual here but, we learned later, in season. We restrained our fire, luckily; they were not geese at all but a dozen lily-white swans, not fair game. In some states, yes, but not here. We saw them each Wednesday for the following several weeks. They bravely approached our blind one afternoon and swam within a few feet, still wary but made daring by the lack of predators. When they took off and circled back over our blind their wing tips whistled and sang as they continued on upriver, a sight and sound that alone was well worth the trip. Later, the largest flock of blackbirds I've ever seen undulated in seeming orchestration across the crimson sky from telephone lines to treetops, an uncanny oneness of hundreds, possibly thousands of blackbirds. Jeff and I spent much of that evening bent backward toward the sky, with birding activity in every direction. Nature spoke to us loudly those six weeks.

Each Wednesday evening, after shedding layers of frosted wet clothing, we headed for a nearby restaurant to thaw our frigid fingers by the fire and feed our souls with a well-earned selection of single-malt whiskeys and dinner. The warm bar was welcoming. I looked forward to those dinners nearly as much as the hunting. One evening we ordered pheasant, a surprise, perfectly roasted and delicious. I considered it an equitable substitute for the many ducks that had slipped past us earlier in the evening.

Put two or more hunters (or fishermen) together in a room, a blind, at a bar, or over a plate of food and they will reminisce, possibly even lie—especially the fishermen. Over a bottle of California merlot, Jeff and I chuckled (ah, I did)

over the duck once downed by both Jeff and another friend, a chiropractor. Bob claimed the shot; Jeff felt certain he had hit the bird, but his unchallenging nature allowed Bob the call. Bob took the mallard home and X-rayed it in his office. Sometime later he asked me to inform Jeff that the X-ray had revealed pellet holes of differing sizes. So Jeff had shared in the kill. But as Jeff pointed out, it was Bob who enjoyed the fine duck dinner that fall with his wife. Jeff shot no other ducks that year. He ate a lot of chicken, I guess.

Usually by the end of dinner and the bottle of wine Jeff and I would be discussing next fall's hunting strategy: plans to drive out to the Finger Lakes region in upstate New York for a guided hunt. Also alluring was the notion of hunting ducks in a land where the sky is blackened by vast numbers of migrating waterfowl; we talked of heading south for Stuttgart, Arkansas. Or should we venture to the Cape again in January for the late goose season?

Finally, after indulging in a cigar at Jeff's house, I'd spend the one-hour drive home replaying the day: sorting out gear in the early afternoon, diligently paddling back and forth to the blind, animated discussion, hunting—of course, complaining about the cold (me, usually), thawing out, drinking, more talk; eating, late-night cigar smoke. This is the ammunition a hunter stores in his memory to help get through the other seasons of the year, which pass slowly. These images are a hunter's companion when he is at work, at home, or anywhere not out there hunting.

Grilled Duck Breasts with Orange, Ginger & Balsamic Sauce

LONG BEFORE RESTAURANTS made moulard duck breasts trendy, hunters appreciated the irresistible taste of grilled duck breast, usually cooked rare. Farm-raised moulard breasts are much larger than wild duck breasts, but the flavor will never be as special.

Serve with garlic mashed potatoes with a little orange zest swirled in and steamed collard greens sprinkled with vinegar and seasoned with salt and pepper.

2 large duck breasts or goose breasts

½ cup fresh orange juice

1½ cups unsalted chicken or veal stock

3 tablespoons balsamic vinegar

2 teaspoons freshly grated ginger

4 tablespoons butter

½ teaspoon salt (or to taste)

1 teaspoon cracked black peppercorns

Zest from one small orange

Start a fire in an outdoor grill.

Clean and wash the duck breasts, pat dry, and set aside.

Combine the orange juice and stock in a medium saucepan over medium-high heat. Simmer uncovered for 15-20 minutes, until reduced by half. Add the balsamic vinegar and ginger, cook for 3 minutes, then add the butter, 1 tablespoon at a time, while whisking constantly. After butter is completely integrated, add the salt, pepper, and orange zest. Turn off the heat, cover, and keep warm.

When the charcoal is gray and hot, lay the breasts on the grate. Grill about 7 minutes, then turn and grill about 8 more minutes or until the meat is rare to medium-rare, depending on your taste. (The time will vary considerably. Decrease the time with smaller ducks and increase with larger ones.)

Transfer the duck breasts to a wooden platter and slice thinly on the bias. Fan out on warm plates and ladle with a generous amount of sauce.

To Drink:

Ridge Vineyards of Sonoma County in California came up with a winner in their 1994 Geyserville. This powerful wine is mostly Zinfandel, which gives it its primary strength, but also includes Carignan, Petite Sirah, and Mataro. A great blend!

Or, from Argentina comes the Catena Cabernet Reserve, by Agrelo Vineyard, a well-balanced wine at half the price of comparable California reds.

Grilled Wood Duck with Dried Cherry Sauce

Serves 4

¼ cup olive oil

2 tablespoons lemon juice

¼ cup stemmed fresh thyme or 2 tea-spoons dried

1 teaspoon freshly ground black pepper

4 wood ducks or other wild ducks

1¼ cups dried cherries

2 tablespoons Triple Sec or brandy

½ cup orange juice

1½ cups dry red wine

⅓ cup balsamic vinegar

1½ cups unsalted veal or chicken stock

Zest of 1 orange

WOOD DUCKS ARE EXTREMELY TENDER and juicy, but they are very small birds. You can substitute any other wild ducks for this recipe, especially if you have four people with big appetites, but you may have to grill them two at a time or use a large grill.

Serve with celeriac-laced mashed potatoes and sugar snap peas sautéed in butter with fresh thyme.

Combine the oil, lemon juice, thyme, and pepper in a small bowl and whisk together. Set aside.

Wash and pat dry the ducks. Split them up the back and lay them flat.

Place the ducks in a nonreactive container large enough to accommodate them and pour the marinade over. Cover and refrigerate for about 1½ hours.

Soak the cherries in the Triple Sec and orange juice in a small bowl for about 25 minutes.

Start a fire in a charcoal grill.

Combine the cherries and their juices with the wine in a medium saucepan over medium-high heat. Bring to a boil, lower the heat, and simmer for 3-4 minutes, uncovered, until soft. Add the vinegar and simmer 2-3 more minutes. Add the stock and reduce by about half, 8-10 minutes. Remove from the heat and keep warm.

When the charcoal is gray and hot, remove the ducks from the marinade, shake off most of the excess, and place them on the grate. Grill for 4-5 minutes, turn and grill another 3-4 minutes for medium-rare to medium. (Add about 2 minutes on each side if you prefer your meat cooked more.)

Remove from the grill, cut each duck up the breast bone, separating them in half, and lay a half on each of 4 warmed plates, breast up. Ladle cherry sauce over each, sprinkle orange zest over all, and serve immediately.

Canada Goose & Fiddleheads in Coconut Curry

FIDDLEHEAD FERNS ARE AVAILABLE ONLY in some parts of the country and only in the spring. If you cannot find them, asparagus tips will substitute nicely.

The lovely yellow of the turmeric makes an attractive background for the green fiddleheads and the browned goose. You could serve this over couscous, brown rice, or even angel hair pasta if you wish. Serve with a salad of red onion, orange slices, black olives, and cucumbers.

Coconut milk is best to use for the braising here, but if you can't locate it, use sweetened coconut cream and eliminate the added sugar.

½ pound fiddlehead ferns or asparagus tips

2 tablespoons canola or peanut oil

¾ cup pumpkin seeds

1 pound Canada goose meat (legs or breast), cut into 1-inch cubes (or substitute duck)

1 small red onion, finely chopped (about ½ cup)

2 tablespoons freshly grated ginger

¾ cup coconut milk (or sweetened coconut cream)

1 tablespoon sugar

1 teaspoon turmeric

1 teaspoon cumin

1 teaspoon ground coriander

½ teaspoon salt (or to taste)

1 lemon, cut into wedges

Wash the fiddlehead ferns in cold water and peel off any brown husks. Drain. Bring 4 quarts of water to a boil in a large saucepan. Add the fiddleheads and parboil for 3-4 minutes. Drain, then plunge in cold water for about 5 minutes.

Heat 1 tablespoon of the oil in a large sauté pan over medium-high heat. Add the pumpkin seeds, stirring or shaking frequently for 1-2 minutes, until lightly browned. You will need to cover the pan in between stirrings, as the seeds pop. Transfer to paper towels to drain and set seeds aside.

Heat the remaining 1 tablespoon of oil in the sauté pan over medium heat. Add the goose chunks and sauté for 3-4 minutes. Add the onion and ginger, and sauté for 2-3 minutes. Add the coconut milk, sugar, turmeric, cumin, coriander and salt. Stir and bring to a boil. Lower the heat, add the fiddleheads, and simmer for 2-3 minutes or until the liquid is reduced by about half.

With a slotted spoon remove goose and vegetables to warm serving plates. Ladle some of the sauce over each, sprinkle with pumpkin seeds, and squeeze fresh lemon juice over each serving.

A Good Goose Day

The arrival of cool autumn air triggers varied responses for the hunter. I was raised in Minnesota, where bird hunting is not only an accepted way of life but often helps stock the larder. Memories of bountiful platters of game birds still linger in my mind. What also lingers is the painful recollection of my toes thawing around the same time dinner was ready.

Minnesota is known for Garrison Keillor's "Prairie Home Companion" radio show and for International Falls, the coldest spot in the continental United States each winter. After growing up in a state that makes a person shiver much of the time, a hunter comes to expect cool if not downright cold, harsh hunting conditions. I now live in the Massachusetts Berkshires, where winters remind me of my childhood more often than I would like; it can be damn cold here, too.

Since moving east many years ago, my cold-weather tolerance has diminished somewhat. But after October 1 my feet are perpetually cold and my nose continues to drip like a leaky faucet.

So, with my historical expectations, upcoming hunting seasons often send me to the latest catalogs seeking the newest in cold-weather clothing. Thinsulate long underwear and goose-down parkas arrived in the nick of time in man's existence and for my outdoor activities.

But I wasn't prepared for the Massachusetts early goose-hunting season, beginning the day after Labor Day.

The growing population of resident Canada geese prompted the state's Department of Fisheries and Wildlife to initiate an early hunting season to help eliminate problems stemming from their overabundance, mostly centering on the tremendous amount of fecal matter they leave behind. After three years of study and listening to complaints by landowners, beach-goers, and recreational enthusiasts, the department decided to open a limited early season to help winnow out the overpopulation. Only a few hundred permits are issued each year the state proclaims an early goose season. The program, as of this writing, is in its sixth year and, according to a department spokesman, has continued to help bring down the numbers of problem geese (and to create a bonus season for hunters several weeks before the actual season for migratory geese begins).

So, of course I wanted in. The first year I applied and received my special permit only a few days before the season began—early September. What I had not anticipated was the weather. When I listened to forecasts several days before going out, the temperature was hovering at around 90 degrees.

Opening day: 92 and humid! Hunting under tropical conditions was new to me. I had fished in the tropics but never hunted there, and certainly would not without being psychologically prepared for it. I do not like hot or especially humid weather, a legacy of my frosty upbringing, no doubt.

I loaded my canoe with all the usual gear needed for the evening, but I also packed a fly rod; guess I didn't take this early hunting season *too* seriously. I knew from previous experience you cannot hunt and fish at the same time, but I was setting out about an hour earlier than I normally would for such a hunt, hoping to cram in some fishing time in advance of the geese's expected arrival, just before sundown.

It was a calm evening, with the sun hanging low over the birch and tall pines. One of the two resident great blue herons squawked overhead, alerting everything else on the lake of my presence—his job, of sorts. Ripples on the surface of the water telegraphed fish activity; swallows dove here and there for their daily intake of insects. With my shotgun nestled in the bow of the canoe, it seemed brilliant fall colors should be splattered about in the maples and birch trees along the shoreline. I quickly remembered: this

is September, just after Labor Day; no autumn colors yet.

I paddled leisurely to a shallow area of the lake, looking hopefully for some spunky large-mouth bass hiding among the submerged stumps. I knew this lake well and remembered where I had caught several monster fish in the past. (Alas, no fish of good size exist here anymore, thanks to heavy pressure and a lack of forward-thinking.)

Since I intended to fish a bit I hadn't changed into camouflage clothing yet. I wore a bright red T-shirt, shorts, and sandals, trying to stay as cool as possible in the sticky heat.

Bam! A splash! I had hooked a rather large fish on my first cast. A challenging fight, several acrobatic flips, and a couple of minutes later I held up a four-pound bass to admire. A good day, if only for that. I quickly released the fish, cast my red-and-white bass popper out again, and—what? Another hit? I rarely had this kind of luck. I pulled in another bass of keeping size—no lunker, but fine for dinner and one of my favorites to boot.

My mind was now centered; I concentrated on prime fishing. As I cast my popper toward a particularly good-looking clump of weeds, I glanced toward shore and spotted several geese swimming around some lily pads. There were about a dozen or so, and they were idly but cautiously keeping an eye on me. They must have been there all along, watching me pull in the two fish. They were wary, alert, heads up mindfully in sentry position but not yet frightened into flight.

What was I to do? The fishing was great, but less than sixty yards away was the real reason I was out there. A dilemma. I decided to reel in the line as slowly and quietly as I could and put away the rod.

A gentle breeze from behind, almost a whisper, was nudging me slowly in the direction of the geese. Something seemed to be on my side this evening. Sweat ran down my forehead and by now nearly saturated my red T-shirt. *Red* shirt? Not the camouflage color I intended, but it was too late to do anything about it now.

I didn't want to make any bold movements, so I slowly uncased my gun, loaded it, and anxiously let the breeze take its normal course. I sat back alert with my finger on the safety and was ready for whatever might happen. It happened fast.

I had laid my paddle down to my left and was about to grab for it to smack the water or the aluminum gunnel to startle the geese and get them up off the water. Sweat dripped onto my gun stock as I inched closer. Another fish jumped too near the canoe, startling me and nearly causing me to snap off the safety. The canoe rocked precariously just as the heron returned, making me more jittery with his sporadic gawking, which echoed across the lake, bouncing off the surrounding hills. I took a deep breath to calm myself.

After a few long moments of our trying to outguess one another—who would make the first move?—the geese suddenly decided to get the hell out of there, before I had a chance to chase them up. But I had managed to float within twenty-five or thirty yards of them, an excellent range and position and, with the birds off to my left, a perfect shooting angle.

What happened next had happened to me only once before and is a rarity among hunters: I downed three birds with two quick shots, a "Scotch double," in some shooting circles. A fortunate hunter might be lucky enough to get one, possibly two out of a flock like that, but three? Rare, indeed. My canoe was laden with an abundance of game for the table: a sizeable bass and three Canada geese. And the best part of the evening was that my feet were not cold, not for a Minnesota minute.

While paddling back to shore my thoughts ran to dinner. I envisioned the table already set and a bottle of 1986 Lynch Bages opened and breathing as I quickly sautéed some freshly dug Jerusalem artichokes with Swiss chard to accompany the tender, dark meat of the grilled goose breast. I would float it on a reduced orange-Madeira sauce and serve a generous mound of garlic mashed potatoes alongside to round things out.

Once the birds had hung several days to age properly, I did just that. Meanwhile, that night I basked in the luxury of a fresh bass dinner, pan-fried and smothered with sweet white onions and washed down with a not-too-oakey French chardonnay. Does life get finer?

Upside-Down Roast Canada Goose

LIKE MOST WILD BIRDS, Canada geese have little or no fat. Therefore some wild fowl tend to dry out while cooking.

In this recipe you are essentially stewing the bird, cooking it upside down in liquid with finely chopped vegetables. This will keep the meat moist and tender.

You may want to add potatoes, onions, and firm vegetables to the roasting pan about 45 minutes before the bird is finished. They will add flavor to the sauce and the bird, and the entire meal will be finished at the same time.

Preheat the oven to 375°F.

Melt the butter with the oil in a large saucepan over medium-low heat. Add the carrots, celery, onion, apple, and garlic. Sauté for 8-10 minutes, until soft. Add the stock, wine, parsley, rosemary, thyme, bay leaves, salt, and pepper. Turn up the heat and bring to a boil for about 1 minute. Lower the heat to medium-low and simmer for 6-8 minutes, until thoroughly cooked.

Pour the vegetables and liquid into a large roasting pan fitted with a lid. Nestle the bird, breast side down, into the vegetables and liquid. Spoon some of the liquid and vegetables over the goose and add more wine if needed to submerge the bird about halfway. Cover and roast for about 1¼ hours. Turn the goose over, and cook uncovered for another 15 minutes or until a meat thermometer registers 160°F. when inserted near to the leg bone.

Remove from the roasting pan and let the bird sit for about 10 minutes before carving. Serve with your favorite potatoes. Spoon some of the juice and vegetables over each portion.

8 tablespoons (1 stick) butter

½ teaspoon canola oil

1 cup shredded carrots

1 cup diced celery

1 medium onion, finely chopped (about 1 cup)

1 medium apple, cored, peeled, and chopped

4 garlic cloves, finely chopped

2 cups low-salt veal or chicken stock

1 cup dry white wine

¼ cup chopped fresh parsley

2 tablespoons fresh or 2 teaspoons dried rosemary

2 tablespoons dried thyme

4 bay leaves

1 teaspoon salt

1 teaspoon cracked black peppercorns

1 whole wild goose or wild turkey, 4-6 pounds dressed

Grouse Breast
with Pecans over Quinoa

Serves 4 to 6

1 cup quinoa

2 tablespoons unsalted butter

½ cup finely chopped yellow onion

¼ cup sweet sausage (or 2 slices bacon)

½ tablespoon coarsely ground black pepper

4 boneless grouse breasts (or substitute 2 large pheasant breasts)

2 tablespoons olive oil

¼ cup chopped pecans

1 shallot, finely chopped

¼ cup dry sherry

Salt and pepper

GROUSE VARY FROM REGION TO REGION. The East carries a fair population of spruce and ruffed grouse. Where I grew up in the Midwest, sharp-tailed grouse, smaller than female pheasants, were abundant. The West Coast is home to the blue grouse and the ruffed grouse (also know as "fool hens" because they seem perilously unafraid of predators). The sage grouse is the largest of the lot, with the male weighing up to 4 pounds.

Grouse legs, as on many smaller species of birds, can often be tough. Some who deem themselves purists—or just lazy—will only save the breast meat. I tend to use as much as possible from any game, preferring not to waste. In this recipe only the breast meat is utilized, however the legs may be simmered in a broth along with the wings, back, and gizzards to make a tasty soup, stew, or possibly a game bird terrine.

Quinoa (pronounced *keen*-wa) is a tiny grain from the high Andes of South America. It is light, has more protein than any other grain, and is delicious as a side dish or for making stuffing. It is prepared and used much like rice or couscous.

Serve this dish with a colorful mix of sautéed yellow and green squash sprinkled with fresh tarragon and thyme.

Rinse the quinoa in water and drain. Melt the butter in a medium saucepan over moderate heat and sauté the onion for 4-6 minutes, until translucent. Add the sausage by crumbling it into very small pieces into the pan. Fry it for about 8-10 minutes, until brown and crisp, stirring and not letting it burn. Spoon off any excess fat. Add 2 cups of water, the quinoa, and season with pepper. Cover and cook for 10-15 minutes, until the water is absorbed. Stir toward the end, fluffing the grains with a fork, and keep warm.

Wash the grouse breasts, pat dry, and set aside. Heat 1 tablespoon of the oil in a heavy skillet over medium heat. Add the pecans and toast them for 2-3 minutes until browned; be careful not to burn them. Transfer to paper towels and set aside to drain.

Add the remaining 1 tablespoon of oil to the sauté pan, add the shallot, and sauté for about 5 minutes. Push the shallot to the side of the pan and add the grouse breasts. Simmer for 3-5 minutes per side, until they feel firm when poked with a finger. With tongs or a slotted spoon, transfer the grouse to paper towels to drain, keeping warm. Add the sherry to the pan, reduce by one-third (about 5 minutes), add the pecans, season with salt and pepper, and immediately remove the pan from the heat.

Mound the quinoa on warmed plates. Lay 1 grouse breast per person over the grain and pour the juices from the pan over all.

To Drink

Serve with a Fleurie from Georges DuBoeuf or late fall's customary Beaujolais Nouveau, slightly chilled. Either one goes well with upland birds, although I prefer the Fleurie.

Spit-Roasted Grouse
with Wild Rice

Serves 4

¼ cup olive oil

1 cup dry white wine

¼ cup apple brandy (Calvados or
   Applejack)

Juice of 2 lemons

12 juniper berries, ground

2 tablespoons garlic cloves, finely
   chopped

1 small yellow onion, finely chopped

½ cup cleaned and stemmed mixed
   herbs such as tarragon, thyme and
   marjoram (¼ cup dried)

1 tablespoon coarse (kosher) salt

1 tablespoon freshly ground black
   pepper

2 whole grouse (or 4 quail or
   4 pigeons)

1 cup wild rice

½ cup (8 tablespoons) melted butter

1 medium tomato, sliced in half

1 small butternut squash or other
   winter squash, peeled and cut into
   2-inch squares

1 stick (8 tablespoons) melted butter

2 tablespoons fresh or dried
   rosemary, finely chopped

Swab some chunks of butternut or acorn squash dipped in rosemary-butter to accompany this repast. Lay them on the grill next to the skewer of birds so they acquire the same charred, outdoor flavor.

Combine the oil, wine, apple brandy, lemon juice, juniper, garlic, onion, herbs, salt, and pepper in a large nonreactive mixing bowl. Add the grouse and toss to coat. Cover and refrigerate overnight or at least 2 hours.

Bring 1¾ cups of water to a boil in a medium saucepan over medium-high heat and add the wild rice. Cover, bring to a boil, and lower the heat. Partially uncover the pot and simmer until the water has been absorbed and the rice is soft. Remove the wild rice from the heat and keep it warm.

Combine the melted butter with the rosemary, pour into 2 small bowls, and set aside. Light a charcoal fire.

Transfer the birds from the marinade to a large platter to drain. Use a substantial green sapling (about ¾ inch thick and about 6 inches longer than the length of the grill) or a metal skewering rod to thread the birds. Tie them tightly with twine or metal wire so they do not slide around.

Rub the birds with the tomato, releasing all the juices. Pour more of the marinade over the birds. (You may also want to sprinkle more herbs, salt, and pepper over them.)

When the charcoal is gray and hot, lay the skewer of grouse and the squash chunks on the grate. Brush both with rosemary butter. Grill the birds 8-12 minutes per side, depending upon the size. (The squash will take about the same amount of time.) Turn the grouse and squash once and baste again.

Remove the birds from the grill, remove the twine or wire, and slide the birds off the skewer to cool on a wooden platter. Remove the squash from the grill. Split the birds in half (leave small birds whole), brush with second bowl of rosemary butter, and serve with the wild rice and herbed squash.

Calvados Pheasant

Serves 6 to 8

THE NATURAL SWEETNESS OF APPLES combined with apple brandy makes an aromatic and delicious complement to pheasant. The delicate white meat becomes tender when braised in the apple essence and caramelized sweet onions. Try it with other game birds or with any older bird that you suspect may be tough.

Serve with garlic mashed potatoes and lots of bread.

2 cups flour

½ teaspoon salt

1 teaspoon freshly ground black pepper

2 large pheasants, cut into 8 pieces each

3 cups canola or vegetable oil

2 medium sweet white onions, preferably Vidalia, coarsely chopped (about 2 cups)

¾ cup Calvados or apple-flavored brandy

3 cups fresh apple cider

5 medium McIntosh apples, peeled, cored, and sliced

Preheat the oven to 350°F.

Combine the flour with the salt and pepper in a large paper bag. Shake to mix and add the pheasant pieces 3-4 at a time. Shake well, Remove the pheasant, shake off excess flour, and set aside.

Heat the oil to 375°F. in a large heavy skillet over medium-high heat. Brown for 6-8 minutes on each side in small batches to avoid crowding. Remove from the pan with a slotted spoon and set aside to drain on paper towels. (The recipe can be prepared ahead up to this point and refrigerated.)

Drain off all but about ¼ cup of the oil from the pan and reduce the heat to medium-low. Add the onions and cook for about 45 minutes, taking care not to let them burn, until they begin to turn brown and caramelize. Remove the onions from the pan with a slotted spoon and set aside.

Pour off any excess oil and deglaze the pan with the apple calvados, scraping together the browned bits in the bottom of the pan. Reduce for about 2 minutes and add the cider. Bring to a boil, immediately reduce the heat to medium, and simmer for 8-10 minutes, until reduced by about one fourth.

Return the pheasant and onions to the pan and stir, covering the pheasant with the sauce and onions. Cover and place in the oven for 1-1½ hours. Thirty minutes before completion, turn pheasant pieces, add the apples, stir, and cover.

Serve the pheasant with a generous helping of apples, onions, and sauce ladled over each plate.

Pheasant with Leeks & Pears

Serves 4

I FIND THE BLEND OF LEEKS and champagne, with the natural sweetness of parsnips and pears, is a combination suited for the glorious pheasant.

Serve with roasted sweet potatoes and sautéed green beans garnished with toasted pecans.

Preheat the oven to 350°F.

Mix half of the leeks with the scallions and prosciutto in a small bowl. Set aside.

Carefully insert a finger under the skin of the bird at the neck, creating a space between the breast meat and the skin. Do the same on the other end, below the ribs. With a sharp knife make 2-3 slits in the skin and flesh of both legs on all sides. Stuff as much of the leek, scallion, and prosciutto mix under the breast skin and into the slits as you can. Combine any excess with the remaining leeks, add the parsnips and pear slices, and stuff inside the cavity. Pour some Champagne into the cavity and truss with butcher's twine or secure with a couple of bamboo skewers.

Place the pheasant in a large roasting pan and pour the remainder of the champagne over it. Rub olive oil over the skin and sprinkle salt, pepper, and chopped parsley on top.

Cover and roast for about 1 hour. Remove the cover, baste, and return to the oven uncovered for about 30 minutes or until the internal temperature registers 165°F. when a meat thermometer is inserted into the drumstick, near but not touching the leg bone.

Serve with the pan drippings and the leek and scallion mixture ladled over the meat.

3 medium leeks, white parts only, thinly sliced

6 scallions, trimmed and finely chopped

4 thin slices prosciutto, chopped

1 pheasant, 2½-3 pounds

1 medium parsnip, peeled and thickly sliced

1 medium pear, peeled, cored, and thickly sliced

1½ cups Champagne or dry white wine

1 tablespoon olive oil

1 teaspoon salt

1 teaspoon black pepper

1 tablespoon chopped fresh parsley leaves

To Drink:

Château de Beaucastel's Châteauneuf-du-Pape (a white Rhône) has almond, peach, and spicy flavors that go exceptionally well with pheasant and with the champagne sauce.

Braised Pheasant with Red Cabbage

Serves 4 to 6

3 cups canola or vegetable oil

1 cup flour

1 teaspoon salt

1 tablespoon freshly ground black pepper

2 pheasants, 2½-3 pounds each, cut into 8 pieces each (breasts halved)

1 small red cabbage, shredded

6 garlic cloves, finely chopped

½ cup dry red wine

¼ cup soy sauce

1 tablespoon balsamic vinegar

1 medium tomato, diced

12 green olives, pitted and halved

2 tablespoons cracked black peppercorns

Juice of 1 lemon (about 2-3 tablespoons)

Zest of 1 lemon

THE RED CABBAGE IN THIS RECIPE, cooked down in red wine, soy sauce, and balsamic vinegar, could very well be a side dish by itself. But here, smothering the tender and delicious white meat of pheasant, it's even better.

This dish goes nicely with a grain like barley or buckwheat. Or slice two thick pieces of peasant or sourdough bread per person, cover with the red cabbage, and place the pheasant on top.

Serve with a bright green vegetable, such as asparagus or broccoli.

Heat the oil in a large, heavy skillet over medium-high heat to 375°F. Combine flour, salt, and pepper in a large paper bag. Shake to mix, and add the pheasant pieces 3-4 at a time. Shake well. Remove the pheasant and lower into hot oil. Brown for 6-8 minutes on each side in uncrowded batches. Remove from the pan and set aside to drain on paper towels.

Preheat the oven to 375°F.

Combine the cabbage, garlic, wine, soy sauce, and vinegar in a large saucepan. Simmer over medium heat for 6-8 minutes, until the cabbage is wilted. Transfer one-fourth of the cabbage to the bottom of a clay cooker or a deep cast-iron pot. Lay the pheasant pieces on top. Cover with the tomato, olives, pepper, and remaining cabbage with juices from the pan. Squeeze half the lemon juice over the pheasant pieces. Cover and roast for 1 hour.

Just before serving, drizzle lemon juice and sprinkle lemon zest over each dish.

Stewed Pheasant with Parsnips & Fruit

Serves 4

THE PARSNIPS AND GRAPEFRUIT juice in this recipe balance with the balsamic vinegar to create a mild, sweet-sour blend.

Heat the oil in a large, heavy skillet over medium-high heat to 375°F. Combine the flour, salt, and pepper in a large paper bag. Shake to mix and add pheasant pieces 3-4 at a time. Shake well. Remove the pheasant and lower into the hot oil. Brown each side 6-8 minutes in uncrowded batches. Remove from the pan and set aside to drain on paper towels.

Drain off all but about 2 tablespoons of oil from the skillet. Lower the heat to medium-low and add the onion, parsnips, garlic, and apple to the skillet. Sauté for 6-8 minutes. Add the grapefruit juice, reduce by one-third (about 5 minutes), and return pheasant to the pan. Turn down the heat to low. Cover and simmer for about 1 hour, stirring occasionally. Add the apricots, grapes, scallions, and balsamic vinegar, then stir and simmer uncovered another 10 minutes.

3 cups canola or vegetable oil

2 cups flour

1 teaspoon salt

1 tablespoon freshly ground black pepper

2 large pheasants, 2½-3 pounds each, cut into 8 pieces each

½ cup chopped white onion

2 medium parsnips, peeled and finely chopped or grated

4 garlic cloves, finely chopped

1 Granny Smith apple, peeled, cored, and sliced

1 cup grapefruit juice

¼ cup dried apricots, finely chopped

1 cup seedless red grapes, halved

6 scallions, trimmed and sliced on the diagonal

1 tablespoon balsamic vinegar

To Drink:

From the Hess Collection in the Napa Valley of California, the Select Pinot Noir has an intensity of fruit and fragrance that shows its strength with the meat of most upland game birds.

Or, a white wine with elegance and acidity really helps balance these sweet-sour flavors. From Italy, Teruzzi & Puthod's great white, Terre di Tufi, is delightful.

Basque-Style Pheasant with Olives

Serves 4 to 6

THIS PREPARATION COMES originally from the Basque region of southwestern France and shows both French and Spanish influences.

2 large pheasants, 2½-3 pounds each, cut into 8 pieces, breasts halved

¼ cup olive oil

½ cup dry white wine

½ cup cider vinegar

½ cup brown sugar

4 garlic cloves, finely chopped

4 scallions, finely chopped

6 fresh basil leaves

3 tablespoons finely chopped fresh parsley

2 tablespoons cracked black peppercorns

¾ cup green olives, seeded and halved

2 cups diced fresh plums (about 5 plums)

Preheat the oven to 350°F.

Wash and pat dry the pheasant pieces. Place them in the bottom of a clay cooker or a Dutch oven. Add the oil, wine, vinegar, brown sugar, garlic, scallions, basil, parsley, pepper, olives, and 1 cup of the plums. Stir, cover and place in the oven for about 1½ hours. About 15 minutes before completion, add the remaining 1 cup plums. Stir and return to the oven.

Serve with brown rice and crusty French bread.

To Drink:

Côte de Beaune-Villages, a Burgundy by Joseph Drouhin or Louis Jadot, has olive and earthy characteristics and medium tannins that make this inexpensive Burgundy a good choice.

Smoked Breast of Pheasant Salad

Serves 4 for lunch or 6 as an appetizer.

YOU CAN BRIGHTEN THIS DISH further by smoking one or two red peppers at the same time as the pheasant and placing thin slices around the salad. If you cannot find mesclun, substitute red leaf lettuce or radicchio to add variety to the green leaf lettuce base.

Trim the pheasant breasts, wash, and pat dry. Mix the cider and the Trinidad masala in a shallow glass or ceramic container. Immerse the pheasant breasts in the solution, cover, and refrigerate at least 2 hours or overnight.

Light a charcoal fire in a backyard smoker (see page 180).

When the charcoal is gray and hot remove the pheasant breasts from the marinade, pat dry, and place them on the wire rack over the wood chips. Cover and smoke for 1½ hours. Replenish charcoal and wood chips as needed.

Remove the pheasant breasts, then allow them to cool in the refrigerator for at least 1 hour. To prepare the dressing, pulverize the pistachios with a mortar and pestle, a clean coffee grinder, or a sharp knife until they are finely chopped.

Combine the pistachios, olive oil, vinegar, dates, chives, cumin, salt, and pepper in a small mixing bowl and whisk together. Transfer to a serving container and set aside.

In 4 individual salad bowls, lay a thick bed of green leaf lettuce on the bottom. Pile some of the mesclun mixture in the center of each.

Remove the pheasant from the refrigerator. Slice the breasts the long way into ¼-inch strips and fan them around the top of the mesclun mix. Drizzle the pistachio dressing over the top, making sure you spoon out plenty of the pistachios and dates onto each dish (they may have settled to the bottom). Serve with lemon wedges on the side.

2 large boneless and skinless pheasant breasts

½ cup fresh apple cider

½ tablespoon Trinidad masala, Old Bay Seasoning, or chili powder

½ cup shelled pistachio

1 cup extra-virgin olive oil

2 tablespoons balsamic vinegar

½ cup finely chopped fresh dates

1 tablespoon finely chopped chives

½ teaspoon ground cumin

½ teaspoon salt (or to taste)

1 teaspoon freshly ground black pepper

½ head green leaf lettuce, washed

8 ounces mesclun (mixed baby greens)

1 lemon, cut in wedges

Cornmeal-Covered Pheasant Breasts with Tomatillo-Tequila Sauce

Serves 4

1 small red bell pepper

1 tablespoon vegetable oil

2 cups milk

1 cup yellow cornmeal

1 teaspoon salt

1 teaspoon pepper

4 tablespoons melted butter

1 small onion, finely chopped
(about ½ cup)

½ small green bell pepper, cored,
seeded and finely chopped

2 small jalapeño peppers, cored,
seeded, and finely chopped

4 boneless pheasant breasts

1 cup Corn & Tomatillo Sauce
(see page 181)

¼ cup gold tequila

2 tablespoons ground cumin

1 tablespoon dried oregano

1-2 fresh limes, cut into wedges

THE PHEASANT BREAST IN THIS DISH is concealed under a cornmeal crust, a pleasant surprise when guests break through the crust to reveal its contents.

I use clay flowerpot bases as serving dishes for this recipe. They are readily available from any garden supply store and are inexpensive. I find a 7-inch base about 2 inches deep makes an adequate serving size. They also may be used for many other purposes in the kitchen: two of them, one inverted over the other, make individual baking pans for rolls, or use them for small pizzas for the children.

Green and yellow squash sautéed with pine nuts and scallions makes a fine vegetable side dish with a salad of tomato, red onion rounds, and orange wedges dressed with orange flower water and extra-virgin olive oil. (You can serve the salads in the ceramic dishes, too.)

You can easily substitute the breast meat from turkey, guinea hen, grouse, or most any poultry.

Brush the red pepper with the vegetable oil and hold over the flame of a gas burner with a skewer (or place on a broiling pan 2-3-inches under a broiler). Roast until blackened on all sides. Transfer to a paper or plastic bag, seal, and set aside for about 10 minutes.

Preheat the oven to 375°F.

Heat the milk and ½ cup of water together in a large saucepan over medium-high heat until it comes to a boil. Reduce the heat to medium-low and slowly sprinkle in the cornmeal, stirring until it resembles a paste. Add salt and pepper, stir, and remove from the heat. Set aside.

Place 2 tablespoons of the butter in a sauté pan. Add the onion, green pepper, and jalapeño peppers and sauté for 6-8 minutes, until soft. Remove from the heat and set aside.

Remove the red pepper from the bag and peel away its blackened skin. Cut the pepper in half, remove the seeds and veins, and cut into ¼-inch-wide strips. Set aside. Brush the bottom and sides of each clay base with the remainder of the melted butter.

To assemble, lay 1 breast in the center of each base. Equally divide the onion-pepper mixture, tomatillo sauce, tequila, red pepper strips, cumin, and oregano among the 4 dishes, completely covering the pheasant breasts. Fill each dish with the cornmeal using a rubber spatula, leveling it neatly.

Set the pots on an oiled baking sheet in case they bubble over. Bake uncovered for about 45 minutes, until the cornmeal is browned on top. Remove with pot holders and set each clay pot on a liner on a larger plate. Squeeze some lime juice over the top of each and serve immediately, cautioning your guests about the hot ceramic bases. Serve extra lime wedges on the side.

To Drink:

Serve this Southwestern-style dish with margaritas made with gold tequila and fresh lime juice. Or try Pedroncelli Zinfandel from California. Its lush, ripe berry flavors won't be cowed by this dramatic dish.

Wild Turkey with Leeks, Savoy Cabbage & Clementines

Serves 4 to 6

1 large wild turkey, Canada goose,
or pheasant, cleaned and cut
into 10 pieces (legs and thighs
separated, breasts cut into thirds)

1 large leek, white parts only, thinly
sliced

½ small savoy cabbage, thinly sliced

4-6 clementines, sectioned

1 cup orange juice

¼ cup Triple Sec

¼ cup brandy

Salt and pepper

To Drink:

I have enjoyed Clos du Bois wines for many years. Their Sonoma County Pinot Noir, with strawberry and fruit flavor and moderate tannins, is a good choice for this recipe.

Chalone Estate's Pinot Noir, also from California, is not deeply colored. But this gem has subtle, powerful flavors. You may have to search a bit for this one, especially for the 1990.

WILD TURKEY HAS THE UNFORTUNATE tendency to dry out if not properly prepared, which is why I choose to bake it in the following manner. Remove the legs about 20 minutes before the breast meat is done so they don't dry out.

Serve with bulgur or your favorite grain, which will soak up the juices. Acorn squash cut into small chunks, covered with brown sugar mixed with butter, cinnamon, and cloves, and roasted, is a fine accompaniment to this meal.

Preheat the oven to 375°F.

Rinse the turkey well, pat dry, and set aside. Arrange three-fourths of the leek, the cabbage, and the clementines on the bottom of a large roasting pan. Add the orange juice, Triple Sec, and brandy. Place the turkey pieces in the pan, making sure each piece is nestled into the vegetables so they will stay moist while roasting. Sprinkle the remaining leek, cabbage, and clementines over the turkey; add salt and pepper to taste. Cover and roast for about 1½ hours or until the internal temperature reaches 165-170°F. in the center of the largest piece.

Dove with Dried Cherries & Pears

THIS RECIPE CAN ALSO BE MADE with grouse, woodcock, or any similar game bird. The sauce tends to be slightly tart. Taste it before serving; if you'd prefer it sweeter, add a little bit of cherry conserve.

Serve with brown rice and sautéed summer squash with mint.

Preheat the oven to 375°F.

Soak the cherries in the sherry for about 30 minutes.

Truss the birds with four 6-inch pieces of butcher's twine. Combine the flour with the salt and pepper in a large paper bag. Shake to mix and add the birds. Shake well. Remove the birds, shake off excess flour, and set aside.

Heat the oil in a large, heavy skillet over medium-high heat. Cook the birds in small batches for about 4-5 minutes on all sides, until brown. Remove from the pan with a slotted spoon and set aside on paper towels.

Drain off all but about 2 tablespoons of the oil from the pan. Add the onion, garlic, and jalapeño pepper. Sauté for about 5 minutes, then add the soaked cherries with their juice, the white wine, rum, stock, orange juice, Worcestershire sauce, sliced pear, and cherry conserve. Reduce by one-third, about 6-8 minutes.

Return the birds to the pan, ladle some of the liquid over the birds, cover, and transfer to the oven for about 45 minutes to 1 hour, depending upon the size of the birds. Baste occasionally. Remove from the oven and adjust seasonings, if necessary.

½ cup dried cherries

½ cup dry sherry

4 doves, 2 grouse, or 8 woodcock

2 cups flour

1 teaspoon salt

1 tablespoon freshly ground black pepper

⅛ cup canola or peanut oil

¼ cup finely chopped white onion

4 garlic cloves, finely chopped

1 tablespoon finely chopped jalapeño pepper

½ cup dry white wine

¼ cup black Jamaican rum or dark rum

1 cup unsalted veal or chicken stock

¼ cup orange juice

1 tablespoon Worcestershire sauce

1 pear, cored, peeled, and thinly sliced

¼ cup cherry conserve, or as needed

Grilled Quail with Red Pepper Sauce

Serves 4

8 quail

½ cup olive oil

¼ cup lemon juice

5 fresh chives, finely chopped

2 tablespoons finely chopped fresh oregano

1 teaspoon salt

1 tablespoon freshly ground black pepper

2 cups Red Pepper Sauce (see page 20)

THIS IS A SIMPLE AND ELEGANT DISH. Quail tend to be very small, so you will need two per person.

Serve with brown rice and also sautéed sliced beets and snap peas covered with melted butter and toasted sesame seeds. The bright red beets and the green peas look colorful next to the quail smothered with red pepper sauce. Garnish with beet greens.

Truss the legs of the quail with butcher's twine and place the quail in a large mixing bowl. Combine the olive oil, lemon juice, chives, oregano, salt, and pepper and toss together with the quail, cover, and refrigerate about 30 minutes.

Start a charcoal fire.

When the charcoal is gray and hot, remove the quail from the marinade, wipe or brush off most of the marinade, and lay the quail on the grate over the fire. Grill for about 6-8 minutes on one side, until browned, then turn and grill another 6-8 minutes. After you've turned the quail once, start heating the red pepper sauce in a small saucepan over medium heat, about 5 minutes. Remove the quail from the grill, cut off the twine, and keep warm.

Spoon red pepper sauce over each pair of quail and serve immediately.

To Drink

An Oregon Pinot Gris, the King Estate — a refreshing wine with peach and melon flavors running through it—is a bright wine for this bright dish.

McDowell Valley Vineyards in California produces an incredibly aromatic white wine, a Vigonier, with a unique palette of flavors that makes it a refreshing change from Chardonnay. Vigonier is a grape that is used in great Rhône whites such as Chave Hermitage Blanc.

Quail Sautéed with Melon, Thyme & Red Onion

Serves 2

THE COMBINATION OF melon and thyme, reduced in white wine, brandy, and Triple Sec, is refreshing and light, low in fat and cholesterol.

Serve with pearl barley simmered in chicken stock and stir-fried thin strips of jicama, asparagus tips, and diced red bell pepper.

Tie the legs of the quail together with butcher's twine. Combine the flour with 1 teaspoon salt and 1 teaspoon pepper in a large paper bag. Shake to mix and add the quail. Shake well. Remove the quail, shake off any excess flour, and set aside.

Heat the oil in a large skillet over medium-high heat. Lay in the birds and brown them for 10-12 minutes on all sides, turning frequently with tongs. Add the wine and red onion, cover, and simmer 6-8 minutes, until the onion is soft. Remove the birds, turn up the heat, add melon, thyme, the remaining ½ teaspoon salt and 1 teaspoon pepper, and deglaze the pan with the brandy and Triple Sec, about 2 minutes, scraping up all the bits and pieces.

Transfer 2 quail to each of 2 warm plates and spoon the mixture from the pan over the quail. Serve immediately.

4 whole quail

2 cups flour

1½ teaspoons salt

2 teaspoons finely ground black pepper

2 tablespoons canola or peanut oil

½ cup dry white wine

2 tablespoons finely chopped red onion

1 cup finely diced cantaloupe or honeydew melon

1 tablespoon stemmed and finely chopped fresh thyme

¼ cup brandy

¼ cup Triple Sec

To Drink

Small game birds, melon, and thyme call out Italian. From the island of Sicily comes the Regaliali Bianco, a great white filled with fresh fruit flavors and a dry finish.

Or, Jean Reverdy's Sancerre, Vignoble de la Reine Blanche, from France. With herb, rich fig, and plum flavors, this white is well rounded with a clean finish.

Grilled Quail with Mango & Peach Salsa

THIS SALSA GOES WELL WITH many other foods; try it with grilled fish and shrimp, pheasant or grouse breast, even venison chops.

The salsa may be made hotter with the addition of more Tabasco or by adding any chopped fresh chile pepper.

Serve over rice, accompanied with a mixture of sautéed mushrooms and snow peas.

Combine the red onion, mango, peach, cilantro, scallions, lime juice, tamari, olive oil, Tabasco, and cumin in a medium bowl. Mix well and set aside, unrefrigerated, for about 1 hour.

Light a fire in a charcoal grill.

Wash the quail and pat dry. With a scissors or knife, cut up the back and flatten the birds with the back of a heavy knife or plate.

When the coals are gray and hot, lay the quail on the top rack. Grill for 6-8 minutes, until lightly browned, then turn and grill for 4-5 minutes longer, until juices run clear when pierced with the point of a knife.

Transfer 2 quail to each of 2 warm plates, spoon a generous amount of salsa over each plate, and serve immediately with extra lime wedges.

1 cup chopped red onion (about 1 medium onion)

1¼ cups diced mango (about 1 mango)

1¼ cups diced fresh peach (about 2 peaches)

½ cup stemmed and finely chopped fresh cilantro

3 scallions, cleaned and chopped, including all but 1 inch of greens

¼ cup lime juice

2 tablespoons tamari or low-sodium soy sauce

1 tablespoon extra-virgin olive oil

½ teaspoon Tabasco

1 tablespoon ground cumin

4 quail

1 lime, cut into wedges

To Drink

Sterling Vineyard in the Napa Valley has continued to make high-quality red and white wines over the years. Their Sauvignon Blanc—fruity and floral, aged in French oak barrels and blended with some Semillon—will complement this grilled dish with fresh fruits and cilantro.

Another great white you might look for is the St.-Veran Verget, a French white Burgundy that is exquisite, understated, and elegant.

Sautéed Woodcock with Oyster Mushrooms

½ ounce dried oyster mushrooms or other dried mushrooms

¼ cup sherry or brandy

1 tablespoon canola or corn oil

½ small onion, chopped (about ⅓ cup)

6-8 woodcock breasts

2 tablespoons finely chopped fresh tarragon

½ teaspoon salt (or to taste)

1 teaspoon freshly ground black pepper

To Drink

One of the best under-$10 examples of widely available Pinot Noir is made by Napa Ridge in California. Its delicate black cherry and spice flavors finish nicely in a soft, velvety manner that is perfect for woodcock.

Or, an inexpensive Italian red, the Miranda Chianti Rufina, bursts with earthy Tuscan flavors and is a great match for this little bird.

WOODCOCK ARE SO SMALL that one bird barely serves one person. I have a friend who hunts woodcock often. He keeps a bag in the freezer, to which he adds just about daily during the fall hunting season. Later on, he pulls out two or three birds, sautés the breasts, and makes sandwiches with a slice of red onion.

Some of us are not fortunate enough to have a freezer full of woodcock, but when you do accumulate enough, serve them with mashed potatoes and celeriac with fresh thyme. If you only have a few woodcock, serve a lot of potatoes.

Soak the mushrooms in the sherry or brandy and ¼ cup of water for about 20 minutes.

Heat the oil in a large skillet over medium heat. Add the onion and sauté for 6-8 minutes, until translucent. Drain the mushrooms, reserving the liquid, and add them to the skillet. Sauté for about 3 minutes. Add the woodcock breasts and sauté for about 3 minutes on each side. Add the tarragon, salt, pepper, and the liquid from the mushrooms. Reduce for about 1 minute and remove from the stove.

Divide the onions, mushrooms, and woodcock between 2 warm plates and serve immediately.

Grilled Woodcock

A TRULY REFRESHING and companionable book, *A Hunter's Road* by Jim Fergus, recounts his many months of roaming the United States with his dog, in pursuit of upland birds. His stories and recipes are augmented by appropriate, timeless quotations. One comes from George Bird Evans, with whom Fergus hunted: "A few fallen woodcock may be located without a dog, but to shoot those delightful little birds other than over a pointing dog would be like drinking Château Haut-Brion from a paper cup."

Serve these woodcock with home fries or mashed potatoes and fresh green beans.

3 tablespoons olive oil

1 tablespoon low-sodium soy sauce or tamari

1 tablespoon lemon juice

¼ cup finely chopped apple

¼ cup finely chopped onion

4 whole woodcock

16 fresh sage leaves

1 teaspoon salt

2 teaspoons black pepper

Start a charcoal fire.

Combine the oil, soy sauce, and lemon juice in a large bowl. Mix together and set aside.

Mix the apple and onion in a small bowl. With a small spoon or your fingers, stuff the cavities of the woodcock with the mixture. Push 4 whole sage leaves into each cavity. With a toothpick, secure the legs together so the stuffing does not fall out while grilling.

Toss the birds with the oil, soy, and lemon marinade. Cover each bird completely. Sprinkle with salt and pepper and leave in the marinade until ready to grill.

When the charcoal is gray and hot, lay the birds on the grate of the grill. Grill for 6-7 minutes on one side, until browned, and turn and grill for another 6-7 minutes. Baste once after turning.

Remove the birds from the grill, remove the toothpicks, and serve immediately.

To Drink

This is a classic dish requiring a fine Bordeaux that's affordable, if possible. The Chateau Cautemerle, a Haut-Médoc, is on the border of the more famous Margaux district and is simply delicious, at half the price of Margaux.

Or, for even fewer francs, a wonderful wine is a Provence red from a fine producer, Mas de Gourgonnier. It is a great find.

Venison, Elk, Caribou, Wild Boar

& Other Furred Game

Venison Pot Roast

Serves 6 to 8

2 cups port or dry red wine

¼ cup Worcestershire sauce

8-10 juniper berries, crushed

4 bay leaves

3 tablespoons mustard seeds

3 tablespoons dried oregano

1 teaspoon cayenne

10 whole black peppercorns

1 teaspoon salt

1 venison roast, 6-8 pounds, trimmed of all fat

1 tablespoon vegetable oil

¼ cup gin

1 medium onion, finely chopped

2 celery stalks, finely chopped

FOR AN EASY FALL DINNER, start this pot roast in a Crock-Pot in the morning. When you arrive home after work, dinner will be ready and the house will smell like someone was cooking all day for you.

You may use venison round, rump, or haunch for this recipe (or chuck if you choose the Crock-Pot method). A similar size roast of elk, caribou, or moose may be substituted.

The roast is best if marinated overnight.

In a large glass or ceramic container, combine the wine with a cup of water, the Worcestershire sauce, juniper berries, bay leaves, mustard seeds, oregano, cayenne, peppercorns, and salt. Whisk together. Set the roast into the marinade, ladling some over the meat. Cover and refrigerate overnight, turning once.

Preheat the oven to 350°F.

Remove the roast from the marinade and drain. Set aside the marinade.

Heat the oil in a cast-iron Dutch oven over medium-high heat. Brown the roast on all sides, turning with tongs or two large forks, about 15 minutes. Remove and set aside. Drain off all but about 2 tablespoons of the liquid.

Turn the heat down to medium, and add the gin. Reduce by half, about 2 minutes. Add the onion and celery and simmer for 6-8 minutes, until the vegetables are tender. Add the roast and the reserved marinade. Raise the heat to high, bring to a boil, and remove the pan from the heat.

At this point you may transfer to a Crock-Pot if you prefer, and cook on low setting for 6 hours. Otherwise, cover the cast-iron skillet tightly and place in the oven for about 3½ hours. Check with an internal thermometer and take out of the oven at about 125 °F., when meat should be pink inside. Cook for about 1½ minutes longer per pound if you do not like medium-rare meat.

Venison Meat Loaf

Makes about 9 1-inch slices

YOU MAY NOTICE that some game recipes include pork, pork fat, veal, bacon, eggs, onions, or wine to add moistness. These are important ingredients because game has less fat than domestic meats. Without them some wild game dishes can end up dry and disappointing, especially to the hunter after his or her hard work.

Preheat the oven to 375°F.

Heat 2 tablespoons of the butter in a sauté pan. Add the onion, celery, and garlic and cook for 6-8 minutes, until vegetables are tender. Meanwhile, in a large mixing bowl combine the venison, pork, pork fat, wine, bread crumbs, eggs, Worcestershire sauce, ketchup, olives, mustard, parsley, oregano, cayenne, salt, and pepper. Mix in the sautéed vegetables and stir well.

Brush the remaining 2 tablespoons of melted butter on the bottom and sides of a 9 x 5 x 3-inch loaf pan. Spoon into the loaf mixture and level it. Cover tightly with aluminum foil and tap the pan gently on the countertop to settle and eliminate air pockets. Place in a larger pan half filled with boiling water. This will prevent the meat loaf from burning on the bottom and sides. Set into the oven and bake for about 1¾ hours. Remove from the oven, remove the aluminum foil, and let the loaf rest for about 15 minutes.

To remove from the pan, run a dull knife between the pan and the loaf, all around the sides. Invert the pan over a plate, tilt the plate and the pan, and run hot water over the bottom of the pan. Tap the bottom with the handle of a knife to coax the loaf out onto the platter. Pat dry and slice.

Meat loaf also freezes well, tightly wrapped in 2-3 layers of plastic wrap. It will keep for up to 2 months.

- 4 tablespoons (¼ cup) melted butter
- 1 large onion, finely chopped
- 1 stalk celery, finely chopped
- 4 garlic cloves, finely chopped
- 2 pounds ground venison, elk, moose, caribou, or most any lean red meat
- 1 pound ground pork
- ¾ pound ground pork fat
- ¼ cup red wine
- ¾ cup fine bread crumbs
- 3 eggs, beaten
- ¼ cup Worcestershire sauce
- ¼ cup ketchup
- ¼ cup chopped pitted green olives
- 2 tablespoons Dijon mustard
- ¼ cup chopped fresh parsley
- 4 tablespoons dried oregano
- 1 teaspoon cayenne
- 1 teaspoon salt
- 2 tablespoons finely ground black pepper

Grapevine-Smoked Stuffed Venison Loin

Serves 4 to 6

1 cup fresh chèvre (goat cheese)

2 red bell peppers

1 tablespoon vegetable oil

3 ripe avocados

1 3-5–pound boneless loin of
   venison (or moose or caribou)

FOR THE MARINADE

6 cups milk

½ cup honey

¼ cup gold tequila

Juice from 2 limes
   (about 4 tablespoons)

¼ cup Worcestershire sauce

FOR THE CRUST

2 cups light brown sugar

1½ cups yellow cornmeal

¼ cup flour

4 tablespoons smooth Dijon mustard

2 tablespoons cracked black
   peppercorns

2 tablespoons dried oregano

1 teaspoon coarse (kosher) salt

4 large eggs, beaten

4 tablespoons vegetable oil

THE CRISPY BUT DELICATE CRUST on this loin makes it delicious. It tends to crumble, so be gentle while handling it from the stove to the smoker and back to the kitchen. The crust recipe may also be used with chops or poultry.

Serve with roasted red potatoes sprinkled with chopped cilantro, and grilled portobello mushrooms brushed with olive oil and mustard.

The loin is best if marinated overnight.

Remove the chèvre from the refrigerator about 1 hour before using.

Brush the peppers with vegetable oil and hold them over the flame of a gas burner, skewered, or lay them on a broiling pan, 2-3-inches under a broiler. Roast on all sides until blackened. Transfer to a paper or plastic bag, seal, and set aside for about 10 minutes.

Peel the avocados, remove each seed, and puree in a food processor. Scrape down the sides of the bowl with a rubber spatula and set aside in a separate container.

Peel the blackened skin from the red peppers, and cut one pepper into 2-inch-wide strips and set aside. Puree the other pepper in a food processor for about 2 minutes, scrape down the sides of the bowl, and set aside.

Wash the venison loin and pat dry. Trim off any excess fat. Make a cut lengthwise down the center of the loin, being careful not to cut through the bottom or the ends; the loin should resemble a pouch.

Spread the chèvre evenly over the entire inner surfaces of the loin with a rubber spatula. Lay strips of roasted peppers over the chèvre. Spread the avocado puree evenly over the peppers and chèvre.

Lace the opening together with one or two bamboo skewers in a zigzag fashion (to be removed after cooking) or tie with about six 18-inch lengths of twine spaced about 6 inches apart (as you would tie a roast). With a fork, pierce several holes in the surface of the meat, being careful not to penetrate to the interior or the juices may run out. Set aside.

Mix together the milk, honey, tequila, lime juice, Worcestershire sauce, and pureed red pepper in a small bowl. Place the stuffed loin in a glass or ceramic bowl and pour the marinade over the entire loin. Cover and refrigerate overnight, turning once.

About 2½ hours before serving, light a charcoal fire in a backyard smoker. If you can, use dried grapevines in the smoker (See page 180).

Mix together the brown sugar, cornmeal, flour, mustard, peppercorns, oregano, and salt in a large mixing bowl. Transfer the mixture to a pan large enough to accommodate the loin.

Take the loin out of the refrigerator and remove it from the marinade. Pour off all but ¼ cup of the marinade. Whisk in the 4 eggs with the remaining marinade. Dip the loin into the egg batter, covering it completely, and then roll it in the pan containing the brown sugar-cornmeal mixture. Cover the loin as thickly as possible with the dry mix, patting it on if necessary.

Heat the vegetable oil in a large cast-iron skillet over medium-high heat and brown the loin evenly on all sides, using a pair of tongs or two large forks (about 15 minutes). Watch the loin; the brown sugar burns easily.

When the charcoal is gray and hot, transfer the loin to the top rack of the smoker. (You may want to lay the meat on a piece of aluminum foil to prevent the crust from falling into the charcoal below, but first poke holes in the bottom of the foil to allow the heat and smoke to penetrate to the meat.) After about 1 hour turn gently, cover, and smoke for another 1½ hours or until the internal temperature reads 145-150°F. on a meat thermometer. Replenish the charcoal and wood as needed.

Transfer the meat to a platter and let it rest for about 10 minutes before slicing. The inner contents will have melted, so be sure to save any overflow and ladle it over the top of each serving of meat along with any of the crust that may have flaked off.

To Drink

Try a California Zinfandel from Château Montelena, a Napa Valley wine of steady excellence, year after year. Zins have the stamina to hold up under the pressure of something as wildly flavored as this smoked loin.

Lolonis Vinyards in Mendocino County, California, makes their wines organically. Their logo is a ladybug—to emphasize their commitment to organic methods. Their Orpheus Petit Sirah is lush and rich.

Venison Shanks

3 tablespoons vegetable oil

4 pounds venison shanks (about 4 shanks)

2 medium onions, finely chopped (about 2 cups)

6-8 garlic cloves, finely chopped

¾ cup full-bodied red wine, such as Cabernet Sauvignon or Zinfandel

2 cups low-salt veal or beef stock

¼ cup tomato paste

1 tablespoon freshly grated or prepared horseradish

4 bay leaves

½ teaspoon salt

2 teaspoons coarsely ground peppercorns

Recommended Wine

Clos Du Val makes a substantial Cabernet Sauvignon, the Napa Valley Reserve. Not inexpensive but solid, firm and tannic enough to stand up to osso bucco's big flavors.

THE MOST FAMILIAR PREPARATION for the shanks of an animal is the Italian classic *osso bucco*. I prefer to cook venison shanks—or lamb, if venison is unavailable—for their more robust flavor. I made this dish while on a fishless fishing trip to Cape Breton Island in Nova Scotia, partly out of boredom (the fish were not biting) and partly to stay warm. Several weeks later, one of the members of the group ordered *osso bucco* in a restaurant and came to me exclaiming the virtues of roasting venison shanks in place of veal or lamb.

Prepare venison shanks on a cold, snowy night and serve with mashed potatoes and hot rolls to sop up the delicious gravy.

This dish can be made ahead and warmed over the next day, or frozen. Simply let it thaw and reheat in a 325°F. oven for about 30 minutes.

Preheat the oven to 375°F.

Heat the oil in a large heavy skillet equipped with a cover over medium-high heat. Brown the shanks on all sides, about 15 minutes. Push the shanks to the side of the skillet (or remove shanks temporarily if the skillet is not large enough) and add onions and garlic. Sauté for 6-8 minutes and add the wine. Reduce by a third, about 5 minutes. Add stock, tomato paste, horseradish, bay leaves, salt, and pepper. Stir together well, return shanks to pot if removed, spoon some of the sauce and onions over the shanks, cover, and bake for 1¾ hours, or until the meat is tender when pricked with a fork. Remove bay leaves.

Serve one shank per person (or divide equally) and ladle sufficient sauce and onions over each before serving.

Grilled Venison Kabobs in Satay Sauce

YOU MIGHT CUT A VARIETY OF vegetables, such as onions, red and green peppers, mushrooms, and zucchini, into 1½-inch chunks (about square) and skewer as you do with the venison. Brush the vegetable kabobs with olive oil and fresh herbs and grill for about the same amount of time as the venison.

If you are entertaining big-game hunters and eaters, you may want to increase the number of kabobs per person up to double, especially if you're grilling outdoors, where appetites seem to be considerably increased.

In the bowl of a food processor add the oil, barbecue sauce, honey, soy sauce, ½ cup of water, peanut butter, garlic, Tabasco, cumin, coriander, cinnamon, and lemon juice. Puree until smooth, about 1 minute. Transfer to an airtight container. Makes about 1¼ cups. (If the mixture remains too thick, like peanut butter, add more water.)

In a shallow bowl mix the venison cubes with about half the satay sauce. Cover and refrigerate for at least an hour.

Soak four 12-inch wooden skewers in water to keep from burning.

Light a fire in an outdoor grill.

Drain the venison. Skewer 4 pieces of venison onto one skewer, leaving space between each piece.

When the charcoal is gray and hot, lay the skewers across the grate. Turn after about 6-8 minutes or when the kabobs are crisply browned, and grill for another 6-8 minutes.

Remove the skewers from the grill and slide the venison chunks off the skewers onto warmed plates. Serve immediately with warm satay sauce for dipping.

3 tablespoons sesame or peanut oil

¼ cup Rhubarb-Orange Sauce (see page 110) or tomato sauce

2 tablespoons honey or maple syrup

2 tablespoons soy sauce

½ cup chunky peanut butter

½ tablespoon garlic, finely chopped

1 tablespoon Tabasco

1 teaspoon ground cumin

1 teaspoon ground coriander

¼ teaspoon cinnamon

1 tablespoon lemon juice

1 pound venison, cut into 16 1½-inch cubes

To Drink

A great Washington State cabernet from the Columbia Valley, the Waterbrook Cabernet Sauvignon is a deep bold red with eucalyptus and black currant flavors and a slightly smoky taste.

Venison Goulash

1 pound ground venison or any other big-game red meat

1 pound ground veal

1 pound ground pork shoulder

¼ cup finely chopped yellow onion

½ cup diced fresh mushrooms

4 garlic cloves, finely chopped

2 tablespoons canola oil

2 28-ounce cans crushed tomatoes, drained

1 tablespoon sugar

½ cup dry red wine

2 tablespoons Worcestershire sauce

1 tablespoon dried basil

½ teaspoon ground cloves

2 teaspoons ground cumin

1 teaspoon chili powder or cayenne (or to taste)

1 teaspoon salt

2 tablespoons cracked black peppercorns

1 smoked ham hock (optional)

1 pound wide egg noodles, elbow macaroni, or spaetzle

THIS DISH IS SOMETIMES called American chop suey and hamburger hot dish, though it's usually made with only hamburger and plain-and-simple tomato sauce.

In the upper Midwest, where I was raised, green or red Jell-O was usually served with this dish. On the same plate.

I have chosen to use three different meats in this recipe: venison, pork, and veal. The goulash can be made ahead and is, in fact, better reheated the next day. Warm it in the oven or on top of the stove for about 20 minutes. You may need to add some water and correct the seasoning. Serve with a salad, warm dinner rolls, and red or green Jell-O.

Preheat the oven to 350°F.

Mix together the venison, veal, pork, onion, mushrooms, and garlic in a large mixing bowl. Heat the oil in a deep cast-iron skillet over medium-high heat and add the mixture. Sauté for 10-12 minutes, until meat is tender, stirring occasionally. Drain the meat through a strainer and return it to the skillet.

Add the tomatoes, sugar, wine, Worcestershire sauce, basil, cloves, cumin, chili powder, salt, pepper, and the ham hock. Raise the heat to high, stir, and cook for 5 minutes. Reduce the heat to low and simmer for 20-30 minutes, covered. (The recipe may be prepared ahead up to this point.)

Meanwhile, precook the noodles for 5 minutes. Drain. Add to the skillet and toss together, mixing thoroughly. Cover and transfer to the oven. Bake for about 1 hour. Remove the skillet from the oven and remove the ham hock and bay leaves. Cut off any meat from the hock and mix it into the goulash, discarding the fat and bone.

Roast Leg of Boar

WAIT FOR THE WEATHER to turn cool to enjoy this meal with friends. Boar meat is dark and firm—especially in larger, older animals—and can dry out easily, so don't overcook it.

Both the rub and the marinade can be prepared ahead and kept refrigerated for up to 2 days.

1 leg of boar, about 6-8 pounds

FOR THE RUB

1 large ripe tomato, quartered

1 medium yellow onion, quartered

4 garlic cloves

¼ cup smooth Dijon mustard

4 tablespoons fresh or prepared horseradish

3 tablespoons coarse (kosher) salt

4 tablespoons coarsely ground black pepper

FOR THE MARINADE

1 cup dry red wine

1 cup dark beer

¾ cup molasses or honey

½ cup Worcestershire sauce or soy sauce

Trim any excess fat and tendons from the meat and make 1- to 2-inch slits in the flesh, following the grain of the muscle (to allow the rub to penetrate as much as possible). Set aside.

To make the rub, combine the tomato, onion, and garlic in a food processor and chop to a fine paste. Add the mustard, horseradish, salt, and pepper, and pulse 5-6 times, until smooth. Remove with a rubber spatula and swab over the entire surface of the leg. Rub the paste vigorously into the meat, pressing deeply into the slits. Set aside.

To make the marinade, stir together the wine, beer, 1 cup of water, the molasses, and the Worcestershire sauce in a glass or ceramic container large enough to contain the leg. Set the leg into the marinade, being careful not to wash off the rub. Cover and refrigerate up to 4 days or at least overnight. Turn occasionally and add more rub after each turn.

Preheat the oven to 375°F.

Remove the leg from the marinade (saving the juices) and drain. Place the leg in a large roasting pan and pour about 1 cup of the marinade into the bottom of the pan. Cover and roast approximately 1½- 2 hours or until a meat thermometer reads 160-165°F. when inserted in the thickest part of the meat. Add more marinade if necessary.

Remove from the oven and let the meat stand for about 10 minutes before slicing. Hold the "handle" (the end of the bone) and slice away from you.

Save any drained juices from the pan to pour over the meat.

Apple-Smoked Wild Boar Sandwich

Serves 6 to 8

2 boneless boar loins,
2-3 pounds each

FOR THE MARINADE

6 cups milk

½ cup honey

¼ cup Worcestershire sauce

¼ cup bourbon

2 teaspoons black pepper

FOR THE CRUST

1 medium Scotch bonnet or
jalapeño pepper

2 cups dark brown sugar

1½ cups yellow cornmeal

¼ cup flour

4 tablespoons smooth Dijon mustard

6 juniper berries, crushed

2 tablespoons cracked black
peppercorns

2 tablespoons dried oregano

1 tablespoon salt

4 large eggs, beaten

4 tablespoons vegetable oil

THIS RECIPE WON me the 1994 National Grand Prize for Best Sandwich of the Year in a contest sponsored by the Pork Producers Council of America. Of course, I used pork, but wild boar can easily be substituted.

This same recipe is also great as a main course; simply slice the meat a little thicker. The crust is the best part.

The boar is best when marinated overnight.

Trim any excess fat from the loins. With a fork, poke several small holes throughout the meat. Mix together the milk, honey, Worcestershire sauce, bourbon, and black pepper in a small bowl. If you have access to a large syringe used for injecting meats, inject a generous amount of marinade into the loin. Otherwise, lay the loin in a shallow bowl, cover with the marinade, and refrigerate overnight for maximum infusion. Turn once.

Light a charcoal fire in a backyard smoker (See page 180.)

To prepare the crust, remove the seeds and veins from the hot pepper with a sharp knife. Use rubber gloves to handle the pepper. Finely chop the pepper and combine it in a large mixing bowl with the brown sugar, cornmeal, flour, mustard, juniper berries, peppercorns, oregano, and salt. This will make a pastelike mixture; if it's too dry, add some of the marinade.

In a shallow bowl or pie plate whisk together the eggs with ¼ cup of water. Remove the loins from the marinade and roll them in the eggs, then in the crust mixture, covering completely.

Heat the oil in a large cast-iron skillet over medium-high heat and brown the loins evenly on all sides using a pair of tongs or two large forks. Watch the loins; the brown sugar can burn easily. Handle gently, the crust will be fragile.

When the charcoal is gray and hot, transfer the loins to the top rack of the smoker and cover. With tongs or large forks, gently turn after about 1 hour. Smoke for another 1½ - 2 hours or until the internal temperature reaches 160-165°F. Replenish the wood and charcoal as needed. Remove and let the loins rest about 10 minutes before slicing.

Make the spread and dip by combining the mayonnaise, pureed avocado, scallions, and lemon juice in a large mixing bowl and whisking together. Slice up some bread, toast it, and spread with the avocado mayonnaise. Thinly slice the meat and pile it high on the bread. Slice the Jerusalem artichokes wafer-thin and layer them on top of the meat.

Serve white corn tortilla chips and the remaining avocado mayonnaise on the side.

FOR THE SPREAD AND DIP

2 cups mayonnaise

¾ cup peeled, seeded, and pureed avocado (1 medium avocado)

¼ cup trimmed and finely chopped scallions

Juice of 1 lemon (about 2-3 tablespoons)

Multigrain bread, for slicing

3 medium Jerusalem artichokes (also known as sunchokes), scrubbed and thinly sliced

To Drink

A spicy Alsace Gewürztraminer from Hugel is traditionally medium-bodied with spice, vanilla, and pear aromas and just-right acidity.

Another option, the Sierra Cantabria Rioja Reserva from Spain, has complex layered fruit, medium body, and a perfect spicy balance to stand up to a prizewinning sandwich.

Gang Shooting for Caribou

The road from Baie Comeau, Quebec, to Labrador City, Labrador, is more than 350 winding, rugged miles of mostly loose gravel, parts of which zigzag across railroad tracks and through abandoned strip mines. But it's a supersleek interstate compared to what my hunting companion John Reilly and I would drive over each day in our weeklong pursuit of the Barron Range caribou.

En route to Labrador City, where we were to hook up with Northern Lights Outfitters, our guides for the trip, we stopped for a night at Manic 5, a modular motel—and the first and only for more than three and a half hours. Originally built to house Quebec-Hydro employees and named after the nearby Manicouagan River, the motel is a mile from the world's largest hydroelectric dam, the Cotoyez la Cote Nord, a 1.5 km-wide concrete structure.

"Glad to meet someone else who doesn't speak French," a man's voice bellowed from the booth behind me as I sat in the motel restaurant, about to order something from the limited menu. Hal Cormany and his wife, Charlotte, were up from Connecticut for an early autumn tour. "On vacation?" he asks.

"No, we're up here to hunt caribou," I told him.

"Yeah? Me, too, if I can book a last-minute trip," Hal said. "But caribou meat? Blah! Worst red meat I've ever eaten. Tastes like shit."

John and I ate our heavily gravied hamburger patties while Hal expounded on his firsthand experience with caribou. Charlotte was working on a carafe of red wine, spilling some on the plastic checkered tablecloth. Julie St-Gelais, the hostess/waitress/cook, sat down after closing the kitchen and chatted with us. Julie is about five-foot-two, pretty, speaks only French, and last season killed a 325-pound moose—"une petite original," she called it—with her 30-06 rifle. Julie is vegetarian.

"You going to put us in your book?" Hal inquired.

"Frankly, I'm more interested in a twenty-six-year-old vegetarian woman who hunts moose than a caribou hunter who dislikes eating caribou meat."

Twenty-four hours later we were far north on our way to being late leaving Wabush Airport, the first of several days of tardiness and disorganization. We were met forty-five minutes later and 150 miles farther north at the Shefferville Airport by Gary Shaw, the camp manager, and Jim Muise, Northern Lights' head guide.

Two other hunters departed the airport with us in a rundown van that drove as if it were missing its differential and possibly even tires. We were to find out why very soon.

"Welcome to Labrador, guys," Gary said, turning around in the frayed vinyl passenger seat and facing his newly arrived, captive guests. "The population of Shefferville is eight hundred. Seven hundred of them are Micmac Indians, and one hundred are whites who baby-sit them." (There is much animosity between the Indians and the whites in Labrador.)

"The camp is only twenty-four miles from here. One of the unfortunate features of the remote camp is that it takes two and a half hours to travel the road; it's quite bumpy and old." That was the first of Gary's many understatements. "But don't worry. The gals in the kitchen are holding dinner for you." We finally ate at around eleven o'clock, the "gals" serving our mulligan stew with smiles remarkably genuine, considering we had kept them several hours past their regular routine. Our backsides were somewhat shaken from the unexpected roller coaster ride, and we were tired. "I'll show you to your bunks," Gary said after dinner. Bunks? I had envisioned post-and-beam, hand-hewn Adirondack-style cabins with private rooms and a sauna. I was in for a surprise.

Bob Brown and Robert "Woody" Woods, who work together at General Motors in Youngstown, Ohio, were our roommates, whom Gary woke by barging through the door without knocking. Three of us newly arrived guests were to sleep here in the two-room camp; one would have to stay wolves—one pitch-black—crossing the river. Ptarmigan and grouse pecked along the road, stirring our upland bird hunting senses. Wildlife was out here, but not the ruminants we'd paid handsomely to find.

"There ain't no caribou down this way yet," said Bob Brown, who became our official sounding board for complaints, initiating the first of many negative comments from across the dinner table. "The outfitters just suckered us into the first early trip of the season." It wasn't long before Bob gathered supporters.

The gals had prepared another hearty meal for the road-weary gang. Tonight was teriyaki-style ribs with fried rice and an unexpected fresh romaine salad, an ambitious accomplishment here, where every pound of food is flown in; there are no roads to Shefferville from the outside world.

Bob continued his oration: "And what's this business about breakfast at seven o'clock in the morning. Shee-it! We should have been out hunting for two hours by that hour of the morning, not sitting here sipping coffee. And on top of that we're busting our asses riding in a van half the damn day." Bob is a determined hunter, outspoken. His friend Woody talked him into this trip, as I had my hunting companion. I apologized to John frequently during the week.

Day two found us back near the same spent strip mines we'd hunted the day before. I found myself wondering if friends back home were having success with the early goose hunting season on my favorite pond, a simple, fif-

teen-minute drive from my home. I longed to be sitting quietly in my birchbark canoe with no endless bumps or loaded rifles bouncing around too nearby.

Strip-mining was depleted in Labrador just over ten years ago, the land, having been sufficiently raped and abandoned, left to mend itself back to life. Driving in and around what was once one of the world's largest open-air mines, we passed torn corrugated tin buildings, rusted out vehicles with their tires stripped clean, and one four-story office building with every window and door broken out, glass scattered by vandals and the strong subarctic winds—the entire scene a testament to mindless, bureaucratic neglect.

The deep, rust-colored mine pits, some filled with blood-red water, were bizarre, absurd. The unreal landscape passed by our windows each day as we checked for caribou tracks in the finely ground iron-ore tailings. What with the peculiarities of the great Labrador Caribou Safari Hunt, as the brochure had dubbed it, I would not have been surprised to see a satyr emerge wanton and spike-horned from the purple mist and dance past our van on hoofed rear legs.

"OK, OK!" Gary shouted from the front seat. "I know we haven't seen anything yet, but don't worry; we'll find you your caribou. Don't get your nuts in a dither."

Gary certainly had us there. We had no choice, being held captive in those run-down vehicles that lacked suspensions or shocks. Dithered we were.

"There, up on that ridge. A caribou!" One hunter's keen

eyes made the first sighting of the majestic Barren Range caribou. Hunters piled out of the vans (rifles pointing up, safeties on) and spread out. John and Jim wasted no time flying up the side of a steep hill in swift pursuit. I held back with Larry, mostly because of my blister, and remained below, moving in closer to the base of the hill. Within minutes I spotted a second caribou, meandering down the hill toward me. Larry, off to my left and closer to the animal, saw it also—a few minutes before I had, he told me later.

I followed the animal, first with binoculars and then through the rifle's scope, cross hairs in place. The animal was on the small side; we'd had varying reports of caribou ranging from 125-300 pounds. After the animal climbed over a bluff and disappeared, Larry and I agreed he had been too small to shoot but then learned that caribou of similar, if not smaller size, had been killed.

Shots rang out from over the hill where John and Jim had run, and through my binoculars I saw John kneeling on the ground beside a fallen caribou. I went up the hill and found Jim gutting a second animal, both legal kills made by John. (Labrador allows two caribou per hunter.) Handshakes and photographs were in order. I asked that we save the hearts, and we set them aside only to come back an hour later and find one gone. Bits and pieces lay scattered, the only remains left by voracious Whiskey Jacks. Several birds had succeeded in devouring an entire two-pound heart of caribou in one hour; amazing, from a tiny bird who nests in the winter. Resourceful they are, wasteful they are not.

We braced for the long ride back, but spirits were higher now; the goal for our 2,500-mile journey had been achieved, by one hunter at least. Somehow, though, the potholes and boulders in the road felt even more intense. We had the third flat tire of the day and filed out of the van. I sat beside the road, took off my boots, and found a silver-dollar blister on my other heel, a matched pair now. I felt balanced, at least.

After a filling turkey dinner with all the trimmings that evening, John received congratulations—no one else had shot an animal yet—and I asked our gals if they would sauté the tenderloin for our lunch the next day. Lunch was superb, and John and I discounted Connecticut Hal's account of the disgusting taste of caribou meat. The flavor was better than most other wild red meat.

Several more caribou were shot over the next few days. A carcass hung in front of camp near the parking area. Two haunches were displayed alongside the cape and seemed safe in the cool Labrador temperatures. Meanwhile, Whiskey Jacks appeared and began their skilled work.

The last day of the hunt we awoke to snowfall. The river glistened, ice gripping its edges. But the snow did little to cushion our ride to Mars, as Jim called the day's newest hunting area, a strangely barren place, almost moor-like, where the only colors were rock gray and snow white.

The wind picked up—to sixty miles per hour, we later

Roasted Vegetable Pizza with Caribou and Wild Mushrooms

THIS RECIPE WOULD BE GOOD with almost any ground big-game red meat. Farm-raised mushrooms may be substituted for shaggymanes.

*P*reheat the oven to 300°F.

Over a large mixing bowl, strip the corn from the ear by cutting away from you with a sharp knife, letting the kernels fall into the bowl. Add the tomato halves and 3 tablespoons of the olive oil. Stir with a wooden spoon to coat the vegetables with oil. Set aside.

Cut ½ inch off the top of the garlic head and peel away most of the loose skin. Lay on a large sheet pan and drizzle 1 tablespoon of olive oil over. Spread the tomato halves and corn on the same sheet pan, with the cut side of the tomatoes facing up, leaving space between all. Roast for about 1½ hours, uncovered.

Heat 1 tablespoon of olive oil in a sauté pan over medium heat. Add the ground meat and brown for 4-6 minutes or until pink (it will finish later, in the oven). Drain off any excess fat through a strainer and set the meat aside, discarding the fat.

Remove the pan from the oven and let cool. Turn up the heat to 400°F.

Peel and slice 8-10 garlic cloves. (Save the remainder for another recipe.) Slip the skins off the tomatoes. Set both aside.

Roll out the pizza dough to a 14-inch circle and place in a pizza pan or on a ceramic tile. Crimp the edges all around. Brush with 2 tablespoons of olive oil. Bake on the middle shelf of the oven for about 10 minutes. Remove from the oven and add the basil leaves. Evenly distribute the meat, mushrooms, corn, and garlic over the basil. With your hands, break up the tomatoes over the entire pizza. Spread the chèvre evenly on top of everything and sprinkle with fresh thyme. Drizzle 1-2 tablespoons of olive oil over the pizza and sprinkle with salt and pepper.

Return to the middle shelf of the oven for 15-20 minutes or until the chèvre is melted.

1 ear fresh corn (or ½ cup corn kernels, drained)

4 medium tomatoes, halved and seeded

½ cup plus 1 tablespoon olive oil

1 head garlic

½ pound ground caribou meat

1 recipe Pizza Dough (see page 182) or frozen dough for a 13-inch pizza

10 large fresh basil leaves

3 ounces freshly picked shaggymane mushrooms, sliced (or substitute oyster mushrooms or chanterelles)

4 ounces fresh chèvre

2 tablespoons stemmed fresh thyme leaves

½ teaspoon salt

1 tablespoon cracked black peppercorns

Sautéed Caribou with Puffballs & Pears

Serves 4

2 tablespoons butter

½ shallot, diced

4 garlic cloves, finely chopped

2 tablespoons brandy

1½-1¾ pounds caribou, venison, antelope, moose, or elk medallions, ½ inch thick and 3 to 4 inches in diameter

¼ cup low-salt veal or beef stock

3 ounces puffballs or shaggymane mushrooms, thinly sliced (or substitute any mild flavored, not-too-woodsy-tasting mushrooms)

2 ripe pears, peeled, cored, and thinly sliced

½-¾ cup seeded and thinly sliced damson plums (or any small black plum)

2 tablespoons damson plum sauce or jelly (available in most supermarkets)

2 tablespoons stemmed fresh thyme

½ teaspoon salt

1 tablespoon cracked black peppercorns

CARIBOU MEAT IS DELICIOUS, not as strong as venison. Some hunters prefer moose over caribou, but I like both equally well.

Puffballs grow in short grassy areas after a rain and are easily spotted from the road because of their bulbous nature; they are round and white and range from golf ball size to several pounds. A word of caution: Never eat a mushroom that you have picked unless you are an expert. If the puffballs are yellow or discolored inside, do not use. (They can be slightly tan on the outside as long as they remain white inside.) Cut one open to check; it should be pure white. Puffballs must be cooked before being eaten. They will keep for 2-3 days covered with a damp paper towel, refrigerated.

Serve over pearl barley (which needs to be cooked for at least an hour) made with some veal or meat stock in the water to help flavor it. I particularly like the graininess of barley with red meats.

Melt the butter in a large skillet over medium heat, then add the shallot and garlic. Sauté 2-3 minutes, until soft, and add the brandy. Reduce by half, 30-45 seconds, then add the caribou. Sauté 2-3 minutes, until browned. Add the stock, reduce by about one-third, about 5-6 minutes, then add the mushrooms, pears, and plums. Turn the meat, cook for 2 minutes, and stir in the plum sauce. Cook until the jelly is integrated into the sauce, 2-3 minutes. Sprinkle the thyme, salt, and pepper into the pan. Serve by spooning some of the sauce on top of each serving of meat.

Smoky Caribou Sauce

IN MANY RECIPES utilizing wild game, similar types of meats may be interchangeable. Here I used ground caribou and I highly recommend it as an exceptional meat sauce for pasta.

The sauce will become thick and, as with many tomato-based dishes, is often better the next day.

This recipe will produce extra sauce, which freezes well and will keep frozen for up to 4 months. Freeze in portions sized to your family's needs. If you use resealable plastic bags, you can microwave the sauce right in the bag. Serve over rotelle or fresh pasta with freshly ground Parmesan or Asiago cheese.

Melt the butter in a deep cast-iron skillet over medium-high heat. Add the onion, celery, apple, mushrooms, green pepper, and garlic. Sauté for 8-10 minutes, until soft. Remove from the pan and set aside.

In the same pan, brown the bacon until very crisp (about 8 minutes). Transfer to paper towels to drain and then crumble into a small bowl. Set aside. Pour off most of the fat from the skillet, reserving about 2 tablespoons, and add the ground meat. Brown, stirring occasionally, for 6-8 minutes.

Drain off any excess fat and add the tomatoes with their juice, chili sauce, orange juice, ginger, parsley, cumin, oregano, horseradish, chipotles, salt, pepper, bacon, and orange zest. Reduce over low heat by one-third, about 1 hour. At the end of the cooking period, remove the chipotle or they will continue to make the sauce very hot. (You may rinse, dry, and reuse them at another time.)

4 tablespoons butter

1 medium onion, finely chopped

1 stalk celery, finely chopped

1 apple, peeled, cored, and diced

2 large mushrooms, diced

½ green pepper, cored, seeded, and finely chopped

4 garlic cloves, finely chopped

6 slices bacon

1½ pounds ground caribou, venison, moose, antelope, or bear

2 28-ounce cans whole peeled tomatoes

½ cup orange juice

¼ cup minced fresh ginger

4 tablespoons coarsely chopped parsley

2 tablespoons ground cumin

2 tablespoons dried oregano

1 tablespoon fresh or prepared horseradish

4 dried chipotle chilies

1 teaspoon salt

2 tablespoons cracked black peppercorns

Zest of 1 orange

Tepee Motel

e stopped at the Lodgepole Gallery, north of Browning, Montana, to spend the night in a 20-foot tepee. Darrell Norman, an artist and member of the Blackfoot Nation, oversees the property and runs the gallery and inn. His daughter, Tina, gave us a tour of the gallery, which houses Native American artists' paintings, drawings, sculpture, costumes, and jewelry.

The "inn" is an open field of about ten white canvas tepees erected in a semicircle around the colorfully decorated main tepee. Sharing the acreage are several Spanish "Bob" Mustangs, owned and bred by Bob Black Bull, a jeweler and cook, among other things.

An authentic Native American dinner was to be served in the main house later in the evening. Tina apologized that the dinner might not be up to their usual standards because of such short notice, but within a few hours a table was laden with a marvelous soup made from the local Serviceberry (also known as Saskatoon, sarvic berry, or Juneberry), followed by elk steaks, boiled beef ribs, potatoes, vegetables, and plenty of blueberry bannock, with enough of it all for at least six more people than were seated at the communal oval table. Each dish was piled high with mounds of food, served family style.

Before dinner Darrell was scheduled to give a talk in the main tepee—our lodging for the night, as it turned out—to a dozen young students from the nearby Glacier Institute, a cultural and natural resource institution offering outdoor-related summer courses. Darrell invited us to sit in.

He began in his quiet, calming manner by telling the students about proper etiquette for visiting a tepee: that is, knock first—as you should before entering any residence, wooden or canvas. The door faces east to greet Creator Sun, and traditional Blackfoot designs are painted in yellows, muted browns, and ocher on the outside of the canvas walls. The oldest design known to the Blackfoot Nation depicts two stars, one shaped like an abstract ear or a question mark and the other a butterfly, which means "bringer of dreams." Inside, women sit on the left and men on the right, and no one crosses between the fire and the owner of the lodge, Norman explained. It is impolite.

Everyone was listening close. Having taught for several years, I applauded Norman's power over the young people's attention span. Dressed in full costume and seated cross-legged, he described the elements of a clay pipe and the importance of sharing smoke with your fellow men. Then he spoke of the United States government's sad and vicious attitude toward a people they classified as savages. Relating his tribe's sorry history, he seemed not vindictive but tutorial, an educator seeking to spread a more accurate and modern-day image of Native Americans to young audiences.

Norman went on to tell of the Trickster, a comic-heroic figure that makes its presence felt repeatedly throughout

Native American oral tradition and beyond. To the Sioux he is Iktomi; to the Winnebago, Wakdfunkaga; to some Eskimos, Apopa; and the Blackfoot, Napi. One of the oldest, most pervasive of narrative figures, the Trickster is prominent among cultures ranging from ancient Greece to China and Japan, from Semitic peoples to African tribes.

Half-god and half-animal — coyote, raven, spider, goat — the Trickster, or Napi, cavorts through community life, leaving in its wake destruction and redemption, greed and generosity, the miraculous and the mundane and, in the telling of it all, laughter.

One story Norman told went something like this:

Napi was wandering about one day when he saw some birds perched on a branch. They were chanting something strange, magical, and every time the birds uttered the words, their eyes popped out of their heads and stuck in the wood of the tree. Then they would repeat the same strange verse, only this time in reverse, and their eyes would pop back into place, in their heads. Napi was puzzled but thought, "This is a wonderful gift. I want to know how to do this trick." So he asked the birds their secret. They were generous, eager to share their knowledge with Napi and show him how he, too, could stick his eyes in the tree.

"But you mustn't say the words more than three times in a row," one bird warned, "or else your eyes will remain stuck in the tree forever."

Napi agreed, climbed up into the tree with the birds, and recited the incantation. His eyes zoomed out of his head and—smack—caught inside the tree. Napi was amazed. He could look around and see grubs climbing up and sap flowing down. So again and again he stuck his eyes inside the tree like little dowels. Three times he did it, the limit. This was fun. Maybe—he looked around to see if the birds were paying attention—just one more ...smack, went Napi's eyes, stuck inside the tree again. When he tried to pull them out again, he could not. It was useless. "Oh, no!" he cried out. With all the commotion the birds up and flew away. They didn't want to be around someone so heedless as Napi, the Trickster. But do what he would, Napi's eyes were stuck. And according to the tale, Napi's eyes are still there are knots in the wood of even the most magnificent trees.

Trickster tales like this one let children hear, in the words of adults, narratives that tell them who they are. With the decline of oral narrative in the West, we have no Trickster to remind us where we have come from and what we bear within, beneath our rational, contemporary minds.

Perhaps telling tales of a people to a few children gathered in a tepee outside of Browning, Montana, will inspire curiosity. And with hope, Norman's strong desire to influence will extend deeply enough into the younger spirit of his own people and help keep tradition implanted close to the soul of the Blackfoot, and that of all Native Americans.

Elk Chops with Fried Green Tomatoes & Macadamia Nuts

Serves 2

2 large eggs

¾ cup yellow cornmeal

¼ cup flour

4 tablespoons butter

2 teaspoons canola or vegetable oil

1 medium red onion, thinly sliced (about 1 cup)

2 medium elk, venison, caribou, antelope, or moose chops, 1½ inches thick

2 small green tomatoes (or 1 large), sliced ¼ inch thick

1 plantain, cut in half and sliced into 6 elongated pieces

Salt and pepper

¾ cup coarsley chopped macadamia nuts

1 cup orange curaçao

WHEN I FIRST TRIED this recipe I intended to use rum, but found I had none. The pan had been hot too long and was in danger of burning away those precious little browned chunks in the bottom, so I grabbed the closest bottle, orange curaçao, to use in a reduction. (You can also use Cointreau if you wish, but for cooking I've found that curaçao or Triple Sec suffices, at about half the cost.)

This happy union resulted in a just-right sauce that sweetly balanced the entire assemblage of elk, green tomato, and plantains. You will appreciate the contrasting crunchiness of the macadamia nuts, which along with the curaçao, helps make this a special dish. Do not overcook the nuts; they may become mushy.

Serve with brown or white rice.

Whisk the eggs with ¼ cup of water in a small bowl. Mix the cornmeal and flour together in another small bowl. Transfer both to separate pie plates or shallow pans and set aside.

Melt 2 tablespoons of butter with 1 teaspoon of oil in a large cast-iron skillet over medium heat. Sauté the red onion for 8-10 minutes, until soft.

Dip the chops in the egg batter on both sides, then dredge them in the cornmeal-flour mixture on both sides. Push the onion to the edge of the skillet and lay in the chops. Sauté for 5 minutes.

Melt the remaining 2 tablespoons of butter and 1 teaspoon of oil in another large sauté pan over medium heat. Dip the tomatoes and plantain in the egg batter on both sides, then dredge them in the cornmeal-flour mixture on both sides. Lay the tomatoes and plantain into the pan. Sauté for 5 minutes.

Sprinkle salt and pepper to taste over both pans. Turn over the chops and sauté for 5 more minutes. Turn over the tomatoes and plantain and sauté for 3 minutes. Add the macadamia nuts to the pan containing the tomatoes and plantain, and sauté for 1 minute.

Remove the chops and onion from their pan with a slotted spoon or spatula. Place on a plate, cover, and keep warm. Remove the tomatoes, plantain, and macadamia nuts from their pan and keep warm. Turn up the flame to medium-high under both pans and reduce the pan drippings by pouring half of the orange curaçao into the bottom of each pan, scraping all the browned bits together with a spatula. Stir constantly for 30-45 seconds, or until alcohol is burned off.

Transfer the meat to 2 warm serving plates and top with the red onion. Divide the tomatoes and plantain between the 2 plates and top with the macadamia nuts. Drizzle the sauce over the meat and onions.

To Drink

This meal deserves a fine burgundy. Gevrey-Chambertin by Pierre Bouree Fils, with a pleasant combination of cherry and earth aromas, surprisingly supports the sweetness of both the plantains and the curaçao and the slight tartness of the green tomatoes.

Another great wine, the 1989 Marqués De Cáceres Reserva from Spain, is a mature red and very tasty.

Loaded for Bear

One balmy mid-June day four years ago I drove through October Mountain State Forest in western Massachusetts, scouting suitable terrain for bear hunting. The roads were bumpy, nearly washed out, and unmarked. This section of the forest was an area only hunters and adventurous hikers explore, largely with the aid of topo maps. As I came around a bend, I saw a man on the side of the road holding what looked like a small television antenna in one hand and an electric box on the other. I stopped to ask him directions and we talked for some time. Al Stockton was training hunting dogs with telemetric collars that emit a signal back to the trainer's receiver. A strong signal says the dog is not far away; a weak signal means the owner might need to start a search.

Some states let hunters use dogs to hunt bear. But some people regard chasing an animal through the woods with a pack of baying hounds as not very sporting. Al Stockton claims he no longer kills bears; he is mostly inter-

ested in training dogs and pursuing bears. I spent some time with him, learning about *Ursus americanus* that, I discovered in the following six months, are not easy to come by.

MID-SEPTEMBER—opening day of the early bear hunting season in Massachusetts. I sit on a soft bed of pine needles with my back against a tree. I can barely ascertain shapes in the dim blue-black of the forest. Dark forms in the early morning woods play tricks with your eyes. What minutes before had I thought was a large head peering around a tree turns out, in the low light of the filtering sun, to be a huge downed tamarack propped against the rotting stump of a black birch. Funny, I even thought I saw two eyes.

It is hard to believe that small berries and nuts are the preferred entrée for the near-constant appetite of a mammal the size of a black bear. But his diet includes quite a variety of food: corn, apples, insects, frogs, woodchuck, mice, birds' eggs, myriad greens, and, in a pinch, the carrion of winter-killed mammals like deer, cattle, and moose. As woodsmen know, this intelligent and highly evolved creature is able to utilize resources in its environment, adapt to new ranges, and cope with habitat changes brought about mostly by man. He is curious—but not recklessly so—cautious, clever, and, above all, elusive.

LATE SEPTEMBER—the Adirondacks of upstate New York. I turn west off New York Interstate 87, heading toward Lake Placid, and into an early season snow squall. I stop at a sporting goods store to buy long underwear and wool socks. Luckily I have a down jacket and a good pair of gloves. And, of course, my compass.

A local hunter in the store points to a location on a topo map where he says he knows there are bear. I drive to the marked location to sit in the light dusting of snow for several hours. No sign of bear.

The next day I set out at 4:30 A.M. to explore another region where a bear has been spotted on several occasions. I set out in the dark of morning and after sunup find slap (claw) marks on the trunk of a huge beech—an encouraging sign. I set about to look for more, but an hour later find myself back at the same tree, having unintentionally circled the area. Six million square miles, or so the sign said, and I had made an imperceptible circuitous dent in its exploration, raising my anxiety level and blood pressure in the bargain. I feared I might have to break out the survival pack—which I never had occasion to use—and I reached into my pocket for the reassuring feel of my compass.

The compass, as it happened, was lying on the dashboard of my car, where I'd left it, pointing north. I consider myself lucky to have eventually found it and my car.

EARLY DECEMBER—Late season in the Adirondacks. I head north again to Lake Placid. Cars cradling skis are everywhere; this is serious ski country. I feel out of place in my pallid, wood-hued hunting clothing.

I stop a postman, thinking he might be able to direct me to my quarry. He suggests I try the Orvis store up the street—they're usually a source for fishing information, but the one also serves as a guide outpost—but then tells me he doesn't hunt these mountains; they're too difficult. He goes north to Canada and hunts caribou, large and considerably easier to hunt. I ask a few more questions, and the kind and kindred spirit draws me a map of an area twenty miles north where he says he knows there are bear.

Forty-five minutes later I'm there, about two miles in on an overgrown game trail banked by a beech ridge and surrounded by snowy pines like a scene out of *Dr. Zhivago*. Nowhere is there color, just white with some shadows. Large clumps of wet mass fall into the virgin white blanket beneath. Hunters prefer this condition because it makes for easy tracking.

I become aware of the presence of other creatures. Countless and varied tracks criss-cross or parallel my path: white-tailed deer, coyote, the unmistakable feathered trail of the ruffed grouse, fisher (or more likely at this elevation,

Smoked Anisette Antelope with Orzo

Serves 4

THIS IS A DISH FOR a picnic—it is best served cold. The meat needs to marinate overnight; the whole dish may be made the day before serving.

8 ounces beer

½ small red onion, finely chopped (about ½ cup)

2 tablespoons anisette liqueur

5 star anise (optional)

¼ cup soy sauce

¼ cup maple syrup or honey

2 tablespoons Asian sesame oil

1 tablespoon stemmed and finely chopped parsley

1 teaspoon cayenne

1½ tablespoons freshly ground black pepper

¾-1 pound antelope steaks, cut into ¾-inch-thick strips (or substitute any big game red meat of good quality)

12 ounces orzo (1⅔ cups)

3 tablespoons extra-virgin olive oil

Combine the beer, onion, anisette, star anise, soy sauce, maple syrup, sesame oil, parsley, cayenne, and 1 tablespoon of the black pepper in a large nonreactive container. Whisk together, add the antelope meat, cover, and refrigerate overnight.

Light a fire in a backyard smoker (See page 180).

Remove the meat from the marinade, reserving the marinade, and pat dry. When the coals are gray and hot, place 1 pound of hardwood chips on top of the coals. Place the steaks on the top shelf of the smoker, cover, and smoke for about 2 hours. Add charcoal and wood chips as needed.

Meanwhile, heat the marinade in a small saucepan over low heat for about 15 minutes, covered. Transfer to a container and refrigerate until well chilled, at least 1 hour. Place 4 quarts of water in a large saucepan, bring to a boil, and add the orzo. Boil for 3-4 minutes or until al dente. Drain the orzo, toss with 1 tablespoon olive oil (to keep it from sticking), and chill in the refrigerator for at least 30 minutes or until cool.

Transfer the meat from the smoker and place it in the refrigerator for about 1 hour or until thoroughly chilled.

Remove the meat, marinade, and orzo from the refrigerator. Slice the meat into ⅛-inch-thick pieces, cutting across the grain. Turn and cut the pieces into ¼-inch strips.

Toss the meat and orzo together with the chilled marinade in a large bowl. Separate into 4 equal servings, drizzle with the remaining olive oil (if desired), and sprinkle the remaining fresh pepper over each plate.

Sautéed Antelope with Cabbage & Orange-Soy Sauce

THIS DISH GOES WELL WITH boiled potatoes; along with the cabbage it creates a kind of German theme.

If you feel strongly that you don't want to use the bacon or bacon fat in the recipe, use canola oil in its place. You won't have the extra flavoring that blends well with these ingredients, but it will suffice. Additional spices or herbs such as caraway, sage, or cayenne will help perk it up a bit.

Serve with boiled potatoes and brussels sprouts.

6 strips bacon

1 pound antelope meat, cut into 1-inch cubes

1 medium white onion, finely chopped (about 1 cup)

4 garlic cloves, finely chopped

½ cup coarsely chopped red bell pepper

2 cups shredded cabbage

2 tablespoons smooth Dijon mustard

¾ cup dry white wine

2 teaspoons apple cider vinegar

½ cup orange juice

3 teaspoons low-sodium soy sauce or tamari

1 tablespoon freshly ground black pepper

Place the bacon in a large, heavy skillet over medium heat. Fry it for 4-6 minutes or until well browned. Remove the bacon and crumble, then set aside. Drain all but about 2 tablespoons of fat from the skillet, reserving the rest. Add the antelope meat and sauté for 3-4 minutes or until browned. Add the onion, garlic, and red pepper and sauté for 6-8 minutes, uncovered, until soft. Add the cabbage (and more fat if needed), crumbled bacon, mustard, wine, vinegar, orange juice, soy sauce, and black pepper. Stir together and simmer for 25-30 minutes, until meat is tender, stirring occasionally.

Spoon servings on warm plates and serve immediately.

To Drink

The bacon and spice of this dish need a hefty complement such as a Bandol from Provence. Domaine Sorin Bandol has deep, rich fruit and soft tannins.

Or, from Alsace, a Pinot Gris Reserve from either Domaine Trimbach or Domaine Zind-Humbrecht is surprisingly rich and complex enough to stand up to heavy-duty food.

Buffalo London Broil

Serves 4 to 6

ARE BUFFALO STILL CONSIDERED WILD? Sure, in Yellowstone and Custer National Parks they are. But buffalo meat is readily available today from purveyors and is, in fact, on many restaurant menus throughout the Midwest and West. Many are farm raised, as are some wild boar, deer, turkey, mallards, quail, and salmon. But animals the size of buffalo pretty much roam wherever they please. Still, they are usually contained within some sort of confine . . . so, are they wild or free-range?

Serve with roasted potatoes sprinkled with fresh tarragon and with sliced beets.

4 garlic cloves, finely chopped

2 tablespoons dried oregano

2 tablespoons fresh basil leaves, finely chopped, or 1 tablespoon dried basil

5-6 sprigs fresh thyme, stemmed, or 1 teaspoon dried thyme

1 tablespoon coarse (kosher) salt

2 tablespoons cracked black peppercorns

3 pounds London broil (top round) of buffalo

1 small tomato, diced

2 black plums, seeded and diced

3-4 fresh (or dried) apricots, seeded and diced

3 tablespoons olive oil

1 tablespoon rice wine vinegar

2 tablespoons Worcestershire sauce

2 tablespoons fresh lemon juice

Combine the garlic, oregano, basil, thyme, salt, and pepper together in a small bowl. Make several deep, 2- to 3-inch slits in the meat, all around. Set the meat into a glass container and rub the mixture into the meat, pressing deeply into the slits. Combine the tomato, plums, apricots, olive oil, vinegar, Worcestershire sauce, and lemon juice in a small container. Pour the mixture into the bottom of the meat container but not over the meat or you will wash away the dry rub. Cover and refrigerate overnight, turning once.

Preheat the oven to 375°F.

Remove the roast from the refrigerator. Transfer the meat and marinade to an ovenproof roasting pan, cover, and roast for about 1¼ hours.

Remove the meat to a cutting board and let it rest about 10 minutes. Slice the meat thinly across the grain, lay it on warm plates, and ladle over some heated sauce from the pan.

Buffalo Pot Roast
with Espresso

Serves 4

2 pounds buffalo roast (such as chuck, brisket, or bottom round)

1 cup sour cream

⅔ cup espresso or strong coffee

¼ cup brandy

2 tablespoons cracked black peppercorns

1 cup coarsely chopped sweet white onion (about 1 medium onion)

2 tablespoons finely chopped garlic

½ cup plain cream cheese

¼ cup grated Parmesan or Asiago cheese

To Drink

The flavors of this dish need a wine that is strong, but not overwhelming. Try a Spanish Rioja Reserva, possibly from Baron de Ona or Contino. Both wines have earthy, coffee flavors.

Or open a Cabernet Sauvignon; Silverado Vinyards and Joseph Phelps both make substantial Cabs with attractive currant flavors that go well with this dish.

TODAY'S MARKET IS BURGEONING with products to satisfy the contemporary cook's needs and wants. Restaurants have no problem finding sources for exotic game to satisfy customers' mounting curiosity: rattlesnake, turtle, alligator, ostrich, or something that may seem commonplace now, baby pheasant.

By all means, if you see buffalo or bison in a market or on a menu, try it. It tastes similar to beef but has considerably less fat.

Serve with roasted potatoes or French fries and broccoli rabe sautéed in olive oil and garlic.

Trim any excess fat from the meat and poke holes with a sharp knife or fork on both sides. Place it in the bottom of a glass container.

In a small bowl combine the sour cream, espresso, brandy, and peppercorns. Mix together, pour over the meat, cover, and refrigerate at least 4 hours, or overnight.

The next day, turn a Crock-Pot to Auto-Shift (or low), then add the buffalo roast and the marinade. Add the onion and garlic. Mix together, cover, and cook for 4-5 hours, until meat is tender, turning occasionally and spooning the liquid over the roast.

Remove the meat from the Crock-Pot and set it on a cutting board.

Strain the sauce into a sauté pan over medium heat and whisk in the cream cheese. Continue stirring until the cheese is melted, about 5-6 minutes. Turn down the heat to medium-low and simmer for another 5 minutes. Turn off the heat but keep the sauce warm.

Slice the meat on the diagonal and transfer the slices to warm plates. Ladle some of the sauce over each serving, sprinkle with cheese and serve.

Rabbit, Goose & Okra Gumbo

Serves 4 to 6

GUMBO IS TRADITIONALLY SERVED over plain rice, so cook up a big batch of white or brown rice to soak up all the tasty liquid in this special dish.

You may substitute any combination of game meats here, but try to balance a light meat (rabbit, grouse, or pheasant) with a heavier, dark meat (goose, duck, or venison) for a variety of textures and tastes.

6-8 garlic cloves, finely chopped

1 teaspoon cayenne

1 teaspoon salt

1 tablespoon coarsely ground black pepper

1½ pounds rabbit and goose meat, cut into 1-inch cubes

1 tablespoon canola or vegetable oil

1 pound okra, trimmed and sliced

1 medium onion, coarsely chopped (about 1 cup)

1 green bell pepper, finely chopped (about 1 cup)

1 stalk celery, finely chopped (about ½ cup)

2 small tomatoes, diced (about 1 cup)

3 cups unsalted chicken or veal stock

1 cup dry white wine

Combine half the garlic with the cayenne, salt, and pepper on a plate. Mix together, then dredge the cubed meat in the seasoning. Set the meat aside.

Heat the oil in a large skillet or Dutch oven over medium heat. Add the meat and the okra and sauté for about 6 minutes. Add the onion, green pepper, celery, tomato, and ½ cup of the stock. Sauté for 6-8 minutes, until soft. Add the remaining stock, the wine, and the remainder of garlic and seasoned flour. Bring to a boil for about 5 minutes, uncovered. Reduce the heat to low, cover, and simmer for about 45 minutes.

Spoon the gumbo over a mound of rice on warmed plates or bowls and serve immediately.

To Drink

The very tasty Angelo di Angelo Super Tuscan-Style Red, made in California from Sangiovese and Cabernet Sauvignon grapes, is big enough to support this gumbo; if you want something special, search for the 1989 Marqués de Griñon Reserva. The year 1989 was a great vintage in Spain's Rioja region and, unlike Bordeaux, this vintage is still available and not nearly as expensive.

Sautéed Rabbit with Rosemary

Serves 3 to 4

1 cup dry red wine, such as
   Cabernet Sauvignon

½ cup finely chopped garlic

1 rabbit, 2½-3 pounds, cut into 8
   pieces (reserve the liver)

2 cups canola oil

½ cup slivered almonds

6 game sausages or sweet Italian
   sausage links, about ¾ pound

2 cups flour

½ cup yellow cornmeal

2 teaspoons salt

2 tablespoons cracked black
   peppercorns

2 medium white onions, finely
   chopped (about 2 cups)

2 tablespoons smooth Dijon mustard

1 large tomato, diced

4 sprigs fresh rosemary (or to taste)

A COPIOUS AMOUNT OF ROSEMARY makes this recipe reminiscent of a Tuscan dish.

One rabbit will feed four people, assuming you will be serving a full meal. Use two rabbits and double the recipe if you've got four hungry hunters. You will then have leftovers for lunch in the field the next day.

Serve with brown rice, plus sautéed spaghetti squash mixed with brown sugar, cinnamon, and nutmeg, and a salad.

Combine the wine and ¼ cup garlic in a large bowl. Add the rabbit pieces and set aside to marinate while you prepare the rest of the recipe.

Preheat the oven to 350°F.

Heat 1 teaspoon of oil in a deep cast-iron skillet over medium-high heat. Add the almonds and stir for 1-2 minutes, or until browned. Transfer to a paper towel and set aside.

Bring about 4 quarts of water to a boil in a medium saucepan and add the sausages, pricked several times with a fork to release fat. Boil for 4-5 minutes, until cooked through, then drain and let cool. Cut the sausages into ¼-inch disks and set aside.

Add the remaining oil to the skillet and carefully heat to 375°F. over medium-high heat.

Remove the rabbit pieces from the marinade, reserving the marinade for later use, and drain on paper towels.

Combine the flour, cornmeal, 1 teaspoon of salt, and 1 tablespoon pepper in a large paper bag. Shake to mix and add the rabbit pieces 3-4 at a time. Shake well. Remove the rabbit from the paper bag and shake off any excess flour.

Lower the rabbit pieces into the hot oil. Brown for 6-8 minutes on both sides in uncrowded batches. Remove from the skillet and set aside to drain on paper towels.

Drain off all but about 3 tablespoons of oil from the skillet. Add the onions and the remaining ¼ cup of garlic. Stir and sauté for 3-4 minutes, until soft. Crush the reserved liver with the back of a large spoon or chop with a knife and add to the skillet along with the mustard and cut sausage, stirring together. Sauté for 3 minutes and add the tomato, rosemary, rabbit, reserved marinade, remaining 1 teaspoon salt, and remaining 1 tablespoon pepper. Toss together, cover, and bake for 1¼ hours, stirring once.

Remove the skillet from the oven and sprinkle the almonds into the pot. Spoon equal portions of rabbit, including a generous amount of sausage and sauce, on warmed plates.

To Drink

A favorite Tuscan Chianti Classico Riserva, especially from the great 1988 or 1990 vintages, is the top of the line from Antinori, the Marchesi Antinori.

Or, Coniglio Selezione from (appropriately) Rabbit Ridge Vineyards, is a delicious California wine made from Tuscany's prime red grape, Sangiovese.

Mountain Sheep Stew with Caramelized Onions

Serves 4

SERVE THIS STEW OVER SPAETZLE. The juices from the meat, along with the caramelized onions, give this dish a slight German twist. Have some crusty bread available to soak up the juices.

4 tablespoons butter

½ teaspoon plus 1 tablespoon canola or corn oil

1 large sweet white onion, peeled and cut crosswise into ⅛-inch slices (about 1½ cups)

1½ pounds mountain sheep or mountain goat meat, cut into 1-inch cubes

6 ounces beer (¾ cup)

1 teaspoon cayenne

½ teaspoon salt (or to taste)

1 tablespoon freshly ground black pepper

Parmesan or Asiago cheese, for grating (optional)

Melt the butter with ½ teaspoon of oil in a large cast-iron skillet over medium-high heat. Add the onion, wait until it begins to sizzle, and turn down the heat to medium-low. Simmer uncovered for 35-45 minutes or until the onion is well browned but not burned. Remove from the pan and set aside.

Heat the remaining 1 tablespoon of oil in the same skillet over high heat. Add the cubed meat and brown for about 5 minutes, turning frequently. Turn down the heat to medium, add the beer, cover, and simmer for 30 minutes. Add the cayenne, salt, black pepper, and caramelized onion. Stir well and heat, uncovered, for about 10 minutes or until hot.

With a large spoon, ladle the meat, onion, and juices over cooked spaetzle or noodles. Sprinkle grated Parmesan or Asiago cheese over the dish if you wish. Serve immediately.

To Drink

Rabbit Ridge makes a Zinfandel that is filled with cherry and berry flavors, appropriately hearty for this stew. Or try Beaulieu's impressive Zinfandel, also with a lot of fruit. The 1994 was BV.'s first attempt at a Zin.

Barbecued Mountain Sheep Ribs

MOUNTAIN SHEEP AND MOUNTAIN GOAT meat are somewhat similar in texture, however some people believe you should marinate mountain goat before cooking. (Marinate it overnight in a blend of 1 cup oil, ½ cup apple cider vinegar, and ¼ cup lemon juice.)

Serve the ribs with French fries or home fries, a large salad, and plenty of napkins.

4 cups Rhubarb Orange Sauce (see page 110)

5 pounds mountain sheep or goat ribs

2 tablespoons cracked black peppercorns

In a large saucepan or stockpot combine 2 cups of water with 1 cup of Rhubarb-Orange Sauce over high heat. Bring to a boil, then add the ribs and peppercorns. Turn down the heat to medium-low, cover, and simmer for about 1 hour.

Remove the ribs, drain, and pat dry. In a large bowl combine the ribs with 2 cups of sauce and mix well so the ribs are completely covered.

You may either transfer the ribs to a charcoal grill and heat them for 8-10 minutes on each side, or until the ribs are warm, or place the ribs on a baking sheet in a preheated oven at 375°F. for about 20 minutes, turning once.

Separate the ribs into single pieces with a sharp knife and serve hot. Heat the remaining 1 cup of sauce and serve it on the side.

To Drink

A Crozes-Hermitage from either Pavillon-Mercurol or Jaboulet is a fine, round wine with gusto. Also, Windham Estates has an Australian Shiraz with big and flavorful berry flavors that's a perfect match with barbecued ribs.

The Bob presents endless varieties of wildflowers. (Judith Franklin counted seventy-seven species.) Glacier lilies, columbine, and bright red Indian paintbrush dotted the countryside. In one field a white carpet of bear grass nearly obliterated all greenery and color, a special sight, considering bear grass blooms once every seven years, if any remains once the elk and mountain goats finish grazing on it.

One memorable morning we rode up to Junction Mountain, an area Ron wanted to explore, and found our-selves in the U-shaped belly of a glacial runoff. Surrounding us were twisted grummholz — small trees blown to one side by the wind — and ground cover like spattering from a paint roller: miniature purple lupine, sky-blue forget-me-nots, white rock cress, red dots of wild strawberries, and yellow monkey flowers that reminded me of my grandmother and her love of snapdragons. Higher up, beyond the tree line, we watched through binoculars as three mountain goats grazed nonchalantly along the sheer side of a cliff at almost 9,000 feet. Ron, who grew up wanting to do exactly what he is doing, exclaimed, "Isn't that something!" in his low-key country drawl. It was a pleasure to spend time with some-one who reveres his work so deeply, with passion.

That night Jim told me of a pool he had discovered on the south fork of the Flathead River, known as the Danahar, that held large cutthroat trout. He described a fresh, impromptu lunch cooked over a small fire, which sounded inviting. So the next afternoon we headed out, Jim and his two horses, Toots and Elliot, and me following on Wimp.

Wimp is a trail horse who likes his pals close by. I spent most of the two-hour ride nudging Wimp as he peered forlornly behind him, wondering where his trail buddies were. He kept falling behind, then breaking into a trot to catch up, forcing me to clutch the saddle horn as Jim threw his head back and let out a guttural laugh that echoed across the river into a canyon and back.

The pool was worth the trip, a photogenic gem of turquoise mountain water rich with silver, fat cutthroat trout. I was climbing down a steep game trail when I heard Jim yell, "Want to see a big trout?" I scampered back up to see Jim holding a twenty-inch cutthroat trout, which I pho-tographed and he released. As it swam away a trout of equal size came up from the depths. After Jim caught another splendid fish and retired to his hammock, I claimed the spot.

I tied on a Gray Wulff #12 and tried a Grizzly Wulff #14, which the Wolverton Fly Shop in Great Falls touted as the choice of game wardens. But light to dark-brown elk hair caddis, about #12 or #14, proved the right choices that afternoon. We brought several red-throated cutthroats back to camp, where they were grilled quickly over the fire and dressed only with lemon. Couldn't have been fresher or tastier, was the consensus.

Other days of exploration found our group hiking and traversing by horseback to higher elevations for the views. Carefully, we rode or walked along eighteen- to twenty-four-inch-wide paths around ridge crests that harbor stories of downed horses and mules. I met a cowboy who said he preferred mules for packing because "they think before they step."

While riding across an especially precarious trail, Jim told me of his experience signing on for a short hands-on course in mule packing. The class packed out for an overnight ride, loaded and eager. Along the way a mule slipped and tumbled several hundred feet down a rocky embankment and had to be killed, in front of the students. Jim shouted to me from atop his horse and across a valley, "What a hell of a thing, huh? All those people watching while one of their train is killed? And their first time out!" He was yelling across a rocky shale slide where the path had narrowed to no more than eighteen inches. I shut my eyes and then very quickly opened, them realizing my mistake. I am not afraid of heights and neither was Maurice, I thought, but when all the horses stopped for an unknown reason Maurice shouted ahead of him, "Get these horses moving. My god!" I was all for it.

A canner is where horses are sent when deemed useless. They end up in Canada and are "recycled" into dog food. Ron Mills had bought Whimper from a fellow horseman who beat the horse, then didn't understand why he wouldn't obey. Old Wimp was destined for the canner when Ron rescued him. By the end of the trip I must admit I was glad he survived.

The life of an outfitter cannot be easy, even though Lass and Ron Mills love it. Up before dawn, coffee prepared first, breakfast later—from then until well after the last ashes dwindle in the fire at night, outfitters must keep their guests comfortable and comforted. I saw how Ron delicately handles his guests when he confided in me one day, as we ate lunch on a mountaintop, that there had been a bear in camp the night before. Although we had all been only a short distance away telling stories around the fire, Ron chose not to say anything, he explained as we sat in relative safety, bundled up in rain gear and munching sandwiches a few yards from a twelve-foot-high mound of snow. Bracing myself against the wind and rain, I asked Ron why he didn't mention the bear to anyone. He told me one of the travelers, Don McMenaminan, an eighteen-year-old student from Portland, Oregon, had expressed his fear of encountering a bear in the wilderness. He would not have slept well that evening; his tent was a few bear tracks from where Ron had spotted the animal.

Back at camp in time for dinner: the menu this evening was macaroni and cheese. I don't much like macaroni and cheese. No, I *hate* macaroni and cheese. "Mind if I interfere again?" I asked Christine, who was following the planned weekly menu. "Just set aside some of the cooked noodles, and I'll put together something for Jim and myself."

As the hot pasta was ladled onto the plates I squeezed a generous strip of sun-dried tomato paste and an equal amount of basil paste in extra-virgin olive oil from tubes I'd brought along. That evening by the fire, Jim and I enjoyed our macaroni and cheese, sprinkled with Parmesan (I do like cheese, just not Velveeta) and ground pepper. "Hmm. This is great!" was Jim's response to my concoction. "Where do you buy these tubes?" At any good gourmet or specialty food store, I told him. "I'm sure you'll find them in Seattle. You should always keep some in your saddlebag. You never know when someone is going to spring macaroni and cheese on you."

What definitely wasn't on the menu was spotting the grizzly; seeing a wild animal of that magnificence is never expected, only hoped for. Lass had told me I would be unlikely to see a bear, let alone a grizzly, in the Bob. In her twenty-some years in the wilderness she had never seen one.

Lass and Ron's eleven-year-old daughter, Schuyler Mills, and I were on horseback and had broken away from the group, which was slow in crossing Basin Creek. We crossed the gravely riverbed, where members of the Blackfoot tribe had likely hidden themselves among the trees 150 years earlier to surprise trespassing Flatheads as they returned from buffalo hunts. I hadn't expected anything quite as dramatic as an Indian attack, but when I looked up I couldn't believe my eyes. "Look!" I shouted back to Schuyler. "Quick. Look over there." I turned around to point out to her the massive cinnamon-brown creature strolling along the river's edge on all

fours. It was a grizzly. Schuyler turned and saw it for an instant. My adrenaline flared up. I looked back to the bear.

My first thought was the closeup shot of the inside of a grizzly's mouth I'd seen at the IMAX movie theater in West Yellowstone. I didn't want to get that close. My next, frightening thought was Wimp. Uh oh. Will he bolt and run? I remember hearing that one other guest's horse, Blondie, was known to spook at the sight of bears. If Wimp reared up like Silver, I knew I would be on the ground, done for. I am not the Long Ranger type. I can see it now in the newspaper back home: "Mauled to Death by a Grizzly in the Montana Wilderness." I was enjoying myself; I didn't want to die with my boots on just yet.

Within minutes the bear turned away, as frightened of us as we were of him, I'd like to believe, and loped off into the security of the dense forest, heading toward Alloy Mountain. No fanfare, no challenging roar. He simply walked on without looking back. Not even a growl.

Wimp remained calm. I was proud of my horse. He wasn't such a wimp after all. Schuyler's first reaction was to get back to tell her mother we had seen a bear. And everyone in the group, except perhaps Don McMenaminan, will always regret having tarried at the stream, missing the chance to see a grizzly in the wild from horseback.

Whimper

Whimper was my eight-day horse,
he truly was a wimp, of course.

He'd cough, snicker, and neigh,
tripping through the Bob, his way.

Wimp and I, we rode on,
over trail and pass, I'd hold on.

My eyes they often were a-closed, the two.
Wimp's: I'm not sure, but I supposed, they too.

Jim and I rode for cutthroat, one day,
Wimp: strutted, bolted, and was held at bay.

Each narrow precipice we'd traverse,
often, I suspect, in reverse.

The grizzly we spotted across Indian land.
My horse, a true veteran, held firmly his stand.

Wimp may not a quarterhorse be,
but the canner, thankfully, he will never see.

Because he was a worker born,
Wimp took good care o' this here greenhorn.

Game Cassoulet

1½ pounds dried Great Northern
beans

¾ pound chorizo or garlic sausage

½ pound salt pork or pork belly

4-6 cups unsalted chicken or game
stock

1 large smoked ham hock

4-6 pieces duck confit (see page 70)

½ pound bacon or pancetta

¾ pound ground pork

1 pound venison or other red game
meat, cut into 1-inch cubes

¾-1 pound goose, pheasant, or any
game bird, cut into 1-inch cubes

1 small white onion, finely chopped
(about ½ cup)

½ stalk celery, finely chopped (about
¼ cup)

6 garlic cloves, minced

1 large tomato, diced (about 1 cup)

1 tablespoon cracked black
peppercorns

6 bay leaves

½ cup bread crumbs

CASSOULET IS THE PERFECT MEAL to have ready after the first hunt of the season, when friends arrive at your house cold, wet, and hungry. Have a couple of good bottles of red wine opened and breathing. (And try not to think about cholesterol levels; one doesn't indulge in cassoulet often.)

This recipe can be prepared a day or two ahead—it's actually better reheated. Warm in a 375°F. oven for about 20 minutes, covered.

Serve with a crispy sourdough baguette and a large salad.

Rinse the beans, then place them in a large saucepan and add enough water to cover them (about 4 cups), bring to a boil, and simmer for about 10 minutes. Turn off the heat and set aside for 1 hour.

Prick the sausage. In a medium saucepan bring 1 quart of water to a boil, add the sausage and salt pork, and simmer for about 10 minutes. Remove, drain, and slice the sausage into ½-inch disks and the salt pork into 1¼-inch squares. Cover and refrigerate until needed.

Drain the beans and discard the liquid. Add 4 cups of stock to the beans and push the ham hock down into the center. Cover and simmer for about 1 hour over medium-low heat, making sure there is always liquid in the pot. Add water if necessary.

Set the container of duck confit in a larger container of warm water for about 30 minutes to soften the fat.

Preheat the oven to 325°F.

In a large, heavy cast-iron casserole over medium-high heat, brown the bacon until crispy, about 6-8 minutes. Drain through a strainer, reserving the fat, and crumble the bacon into small pieces. Set both aside.

Remove the salt pork and chorizo from the refrigerator.

Remove the confit from the fat and cut away or pull off all the meat from the bone. Cut the meat into bite-size pieces and set aside.

Return about 2 tablespoons of bacon fat to the casserole, add the ground pork, and sauté for 3-4 minutes, until browned. Remove, drain, and set the ground pork aside. Add the salt pork and chorizo to the casserole and sauté for 6-8 minutes, stirring constantly. Add another tablespoon of the reserved bacon fat, the venison, and the game bird meat and sauté for 3-4 minutes, until browned. Add more bacon fat if necessary and add the onion, celery, garlic, tomato, and pepper, stirring constantly. Sauté for about 5 minutes.

Remove the beans from the heat, drain, and reserve any liquid.

Remove the casserole from the heat and transfer the contents to a large bowl or container. You will now layer everything back into the casserole. Remove the ham hock from the bean pot and set it in the center of the casserole. Pick out the salt pork and lay it in the bottom of the casserole and around the ham hock. Ladle a layer of beans over the salt pork, covering the bottom of the pot. Over the beans, ladle a ¼-inch layer of the meat mixture, some crisped bacon, and some ground pork. Repeat similar layers of beans, meat mixture, bacon and ground pork, continuing until the casserole is three-fourths filled. Lay all of the duck confit pieces on top and push them down into the mixture. Push down the bay leaves and sprinkle the bread crumbs over the top. Drizzle 1-2 tablespoons of any remaining bacon fat over the crumbs and pour in 1½ cups juice remaining from the beans and additional stock (if needed) until the casserole is about three-fourths filled with liquid. (The recipe may be made one day ahead up to this point and refrigerated.)

Cover and place in the oven for 2 hours. Remove, uncover, and return to the oven to finish baking for 30 minutes.

Remove the casserole from the oven and with a pair of tongs or a large fork, remove the ham hock from the center of the beans. Cut off any meat from the bone and return it to the casserole. Discard the fat and bone. Remove the bay leaves.

Ladle cassoulet containing equal portions of confit onto warm plates and serve immediately.

Black Bean, Wild Game & Corn Chili

Serves 4 to 5

¾ cup dried black beans

1 cup unsalted veal or meat stock

12 ounces beer

½ cup dry sherry or red wine

2 tablespoons Worcestershire sauce

2 tablespoons vegetable oil

1 medium yellow onion, finely chopped (about 1 cup)

4 garlic cloves, minced

¼ red bell pepper, seeded and finely chopped

¾ pound antelope, cut into 1-inch chunks

¾ pound ground caribou

1 28-ounce can stewed tomatoes

1½ tablespoons Old Bay Seasoning

1 teaspoon cayenne

2 tablespoons dried oregano

2 teaspoons ground cumin

1 teaspoon salt

1 tablespoon cracked black peppercorns

¾ cup corn kernels, fresh or canned

I USED GROUND CARIBOU and antelope chunks for this recipe, but you can use any combination of big game that you choose.

As with many tomato dishes, chili is best made ahead one day and reheated the next.

Combine the beans and 2 cups of water in a large saucepan over medium-high heat. Bring to a boil for 2 minutes and then shut off heat. Cover and let the beans sit for one hour, then drain. Return the beans to pan, add 2 cups of fresh water, the stock, beer, sherry, and Worcestershire sauce. Cover, bring to a boil, reduce the heat to medium-low, and cook for about 1½ hours, adding more water if necessary.

Heat 1 tablespoon of the oil in a large cast-iron skillet over medium-high heat and add the onion, garlic, and red pepper. Sauté for 4-5 minutes, until soft. Transfer to a bowl and set aside.

Heat the remaining 1 tablespoon of oil in the skillet and add the chunks of antelope. Brown on all sides for 3-4 minutes. With a slotted spoon, transfer to a bowl and set aside.

Add the ground caribou to the skillet and brown it for 2-3 minutes. Add the tomatoes with their juice, Old Bay Seasoning, cayenne, oregano, cumin, salt, and pepper. Return the onion, garlic, red pepper, and antelope chunks to the skillet. Stir, cover, and bring to a boil. Reduce the heat to medium-low and simmer for about 1 hour.

Drain the beans, reserving any liquid. Add the beans and corn kernels to the skillet, stir, cover, and simmer for about 30 minutes. Add some liquid from the beans if the chili gets too dry.

Serve immediately or refrigerate in a nonmetallic container and reheat the next day.

Shepherd's Pie

TRADITIONALLY, SHEPHERD'S PIE IS made with finely chopped meat or hash. The addition of pea soup creates a nontraditional sweet vegetable base for the casserole and adds flavor.

You will need 2 cups of homemade mashed potatoes for this recipe; it's a good place to use up leftovers.

Preheat the oven to 350°F.

Heat the oil in a large cast-iron skillet over medium heat. Add the onion, carrot, and garlic. Sauté for 2-3 minutes, until soft, and add the meat chunks. Sauté for 6-8 minutes or until the meat is browned on all sides. Combine the soup and milk and add to the pan. Stir, cover, and place the skillet in the oven to bake for about 30 minutes.

Remove the skillet from the oven. Turn up the oven to 425°F. Sprinkle the peas and tomato over the meat and, with a rubber spatula, spread the mashed potatoes over entire pan. Drizzle with melted butter and sprinkle with salt, pepper, and parsley. Return the uncovered skillet to the oven and bake for another 10-15 minutes or until the potatoes are browned.

Remove the skillet from the oven and spoon servings onto warmed plates. Serve immediately, along with a salad and bread.

1 tablespoon vegetable oil

1 small white onion, coarsely chopped (about ½ cup)

1 medium carrot, shredded (about ½ cup)

3 garlic cloves, finely chopped

1½ pounds venison, elk, moose or caribou, cut into 1½-inch cubes

1½ cups French Canadian Pea Soup (see page 12) or 1 can split pea soup

½ cup milk

1 cup fresh or frozen peas

1 plum tomato, diced (about ½ cup)

2 cups mashed potatoes

2 tablespoons melted butter

½ teaspoon salt

1 tablespoon coarsely ground black pepper

1 tablespoon freshly chopped parsley

To Drink

Château Souverain, Beringer Vineyards' "second label," makes a delicious red Zinfandel that's quite suitable for shepherd's pie.

Or try a red Côtes de Provence from Domaine Sorin. Like most Provençal reds, this one is inexpensive, full of herbs and fruit flavors, and good for the soul.

Venison, Elk & Wild Duck Stew

Serves 4 to 6

I MADE THIS STEW IN MONTANA one November after returning from a cold day of duck hunting with two ducks in hand. Earlier, a hunting companion had given me some fresh elk steaks and I also had a piece of venison I wanted to use. You can, of course, use any combination of wild game.

1½ pounds venison

1 pound elk meat

1 pound wild duck breast meat

FOR THE MARINADE

6 ounces beer (¾ cup)

¼ cup yellow mustard

2 tablespoons Worcestershire sauce

1 small onion, chopped

4 garlic cloves, diced

6 juniper berries, crushed

2 tablespoons fresh or dried oregano

1 teaspoon salt

2 teaspoons black pepper

FOR THE STEW

2 small carrots, cut into chunks

2 large parsnips, cut into chunks

2 medium potatoes, peeled and cut into chunks

1 tablespoon canola or vegetable oil

½ small red onion, coarsely chopped

1 cup dry red wine

1 apple, peeled, cored, and sliced

1 small tomato, diced

2 teaspoons cayenne

1 tablespoon nutmeg

Cut the venison and elk into 2-inch cubes and the duck breast into 1-inch pieces. Set aside. Combine the beer, mustard, Worcestershire sauce, onion, cloves, juniper berries, oregano, salt, and pepper in a large nonreactive bowl. Whisk together. Add all the meat, stir, cover, and refrigerate for at least 2 hours or overnight.

Preheat the oven to 400°F.

Bring 4 quarts of water to a boil in a large saucepan. Add the carrots, parsnips, and potatoes. Boil for about 5 minutes or until the vegetables are still firm and not completely cooked. Drain and set the vegetables aside.

Remove the meat from the refrigerator, drain, reserving the marinade.

Heat the oil in a large cast-iron skillet over medium-high heat and add the meat. Sauté, stirring occasionally, for 6-8 minutes, until browned. Add the onion, sauté for 5 minutes, and add the wine. Simmer for 3 minutes, then add the cooked vegetables, apple, tomato, cayenne, nutmeg, and reserved marinade. Stir together, cover, and place in the oven for 1½ hours.

Serve with good crusty bread to soak up the sauce.

To Drink

This stew goes nicely with an Italian Barolo such as Batasiolo, which is generous in fruit, not too tannic, and finishes with a rich but not overly oaky flavor. Or, you can't go wrong with a California Zinfandel. Rosenblum Vineyards offers an inexpensive cuvée or single vineyard Zin that complements the diverse ingredients in this stew.

Vegetable
Accompaniments

Sausage, Apple & Onion Stuffing

1 pound venison sausage

1 tablespoon canola or corn oil

2 large onions, finely chopped

4 medium apples, peeled, cored, thinly sliced

1½ cups bread crumbs

1 cup fresh apple cider

2 eggs, beaten

2 tablespoons smooth Dijon mustard

1 cup finely chopped fresh or ½ cup dried apricots

½ cup coarsely chopped pecans, hazelnuts, or pine nuts

¼ cup chopped fresh sage leaves

½ teaspoon salt

1 tablespoon freshly ground black pepper

YOU CAN STUFF ANY GAME BIRD, but I recommend instead either surrounding the bird with the stuffing or baking it separately. I don't believe the stuffing benefits much by being cooked inside the bird; when the cavity is filled, the bird cannot cook from the inside out—only from the outside in. With an open cavity, you will find a faster and more even cooking.

This recipe makes enough stuffing for 1 large or 2-3 small birds.

Preheat the oven to 350°F.

Heat the oil in a medium sauté pan over medium-high heat. Crumble the sausage into the pan and add the onions and apples. Sauté 8-10 minutes, uncovered, stirring frequently. Remove from the heat, drain any excess oil, and set aside.

In a large mixing bowl combine the bread crumbs, cider, eggs, mustard, apricots, nuts, sage, and salt and pepper. Stir together, add the sausage mixture, and stir thoroughly.

Bake in a covered casserole for 30-40 minutes, until thoroughly warmed.

White Bean Puree

Serves 4 to 6

THIS PUREE—TUSCAN IN CONCEPT—can accompany many dishes. If you don't want to bother cooking the beans, substitute canned cannelini or other white beans. Simmer the canned beans with pork bones, about 1 cup stock, and garlic for about 15 minutes before pureeing with the vegetables.

Place 2 cups of water in a large saucepan over medium-high heat. Add the beans, cover, and bring to a boil. Cook for about 5 minutes, then turn off the heat and set aside for 1 hour.

Drain the beans, add 2 cups of water, 2 cups of the stock, the garlic, pork bones, and sage. Bring to a boil, reduce the heat to medium-low, and simmer, covered, for 2 hours, adding more stock as needed. During the last 20 minutes, slide the cover to one side so all the liquid cooks out.

Heat the oil in a medium sauté pan over medium-high heat. Remove half of the garlic from the beans and add to the pan along with the onion and carrot. Sauté for 5-6 minutes, until soft. Add the tomatoes and pepper and sauté for 3-4 minutes more, until tender.

Transfer to the bowl of a food processor equipped with a metal blade. Add three-quarters of the cooked beans and puree for about 1 minute. Scrape down the sides of the processor and continue to puree for about 15 seconds.

Mound the whole beans on top of the pureed beans. Sprinkle with additional salt, pepper, and olive oil, if desired, before serving.

16 ounces dried Great Northern beans

4 cups low-salt veal or chicken stock, or as needed

10-12 garlic cloves, peeled

1 pound smoked pork neck bones or hocks or ½ cup diced ham

1 tablespoon chopped fresh sage

2 tablespoons olive oil

1 small onion, finely chopped (about ½ cup)

1 small carrot, finely chopped (about ½ cup)

2 medium plum tomatoes, diced

1 tablespoon coarsely ground black pepper

Three Vegetable Purees

Serves 4 to 6

THESE PUREES MAKE attractive accompaniments when served with steamed or sautéed vegetables of a different color

FOR THE CARROT PUREE

6 medium carrots, cut into 1-inch chunks (about 3 cups)

8 tablespoons (½ cup) butter

1 small Vidalia onion, chopped (about ½ cup)

¼ cup minced fresh ginger

¼ cup orange juice

1 tablespoon lime juice

1 teaspoon salt

1 teaspoon ground white pepper

Zest of ½ orange

Zest of ½ lime

FOR THE ARTICHOKE PUREE

5-6 whole artichokes

½ cup melted butter

4 teaspoons chopped fresh dill

Salt and pepper

Lemon wedges, for garnish

FOR THE PARSNIP PUREE

4 cups peeled and chopped parsnips

½ cup melted unsalted butter

Juice of ½ small orange (¼ cup)

Salt and pepper

Zest of 1 orange

CARROT-GINGER PUREE WITH ORANGE & LIME ZEST: Bring about 3 quarts of water to a boil in a large saucepan. Cook the carrots until soft, 10-12 minutes. Drain and set aside. Melt the butter in a medium skillet, add the onion, and sauté for 6-8 minutes, until onion is translucent. Add the ginger, orange juice, lime juice, salt, pepper, and orange and lime zest and reduce by one-half, about 4 minutes.

Blend the carrots in the bowl of a food processor for 1-2 minutes, or until the carrots are finely chopped. Scrape up the contents of the sauté pan with a rubber spatula and combine with the carrots in the food processor. Puree for 2-3 minutes, or until the mixture is smooth. Serve immediately.

ARTICHOKE HEART PUREE: Trim the stem from each artichoke and boil the artichokes in 4 quarts of water over medium-high heat for about 20 minutes. Peel away all the leaves and, with a teaspoon, scrape away the prickly fibers from the heart. Quarter each heart.

While still warm, puree the artichoke hearts with the butter, dill, and salt and pepper to taste in a food processor until smooth, 2-3 minutes. Scrape down the sides of the bowl and pulse several more times. Serve immediately with 2 or 3 artichoke leaves and lemon wedges as garnish.

PARSNIP PUREE WITH ORANGE ZEST: Boil the parsnips in a large saucepan over medium-high heat for 12-14 minutes, or until a sharp knife pierces them easily. Drain and puree in a food processor for 2-3 minutes, until smooth. Scrape down the sides of the bowl, pulse 4-5 times, and add the butter, orange juice, salt and pepper to taste, and orange zest. Puree for another 1-2 minutes or until smooth. Serve immediately.

Song of the North

innesota air almost crackles. It feels crispy clean, as it should in this northern clime. It is quiet. It shifts slightly to allow the tips of the mighty spruce and fir to waver, whispering each to each.

In early autumn, as it is now, the forest grows cool— especially on the north shore of the glacial lake where I've made camp. A red squirrel races up a paper birch. With firm-footed agility it skips over to an adjoining red oak, probably to procure its winter cache of acorns.

The squirrel chatters loudly, metallically, two quarters being clicked together. It is scolding a hermit thrush that has intruded on its territory. After a brief, animated exchange the bird flees skyward, escaping the squirrel's challenge. The small furry creature descends the tree, no doubt feeling triumphant. It bounds off, not noticing me. A heron passes overhead, a slow, lanky bird that cranks its head sideways, aloof, before disappearing over the treetops.

My tent is pitched near a protective cover of sweet viburnum, and I lay a bed in preparation for the snapping fire I'll light after dark to cook my freshly caught trout. I gather balsam needles for a pillow, anticipating how it will be to nestle my head in the fragrant scent.

The lake is calm today. I rig my fly rod and cast to the rise of a fish twenty yards from shore. The line lies out flat, disturbing the mirrorlike surface. A ringlet of ripples overlaps the fish's wake in a shimmering moiré. My caddis traverses the last wake and settles down, lonely out there.

A crimson maple leaf flutters from overhead, settling on the rich blue-green surface, alongside the isolated fly. Towering pine, canoe birch, and hobblebush line the far shore, a brush stroke of silver-blue highlighting the water's edge. Beyond lies a swath of dark vermilion playing off the less intense purples of the distant haze.

My minuscule fly remains a motionless speck on the flat water and I hold onto the image for as long as possible while the sun's diminishing presence tempers the richly colored picture to near black. I'm always fearful that a fish might take my fly and ruin the frame.

The picture fades undisturbed, though, and I meander back through darkened woods for a fishless meal beside the fire. I do not mind. The images I can re-create when I shut my eyes are reward enough.

But if I could capture just one aspect of this awe-inspiring wilderness at the source of the Mississippi, it would not be the sight of the tree-rich hills rising majestically from the bowels of the earth or the sweet-spicy fragrance of balsam fir, the essence of a northern forest. It would be the wonderful gargling sound of the loon, the black-and-white feathered prince of northern waters whose humorous yodelings inspire tranquillity and instill good, night feelings. I lie awake a long while listening as somewhere on the shore close by a feathered neck expands and contracts in melodious exchange. Across the dim waters another loon dives, surfaces, shakes its sleek head vigorously from side to side, and returns the song.

Accepted as a guest in the north woods, I relent to its vigorous charms. As I drift off to sleep an a cappella chorus of loons charms the darkness. Evening chatter gradually gives way to nightfall as every creature listens attentively for the loon, Director of Night Sounds. I sleep well, dreaming in black and white, of course.

By morning the croony loons are silent but still visible on the water. The forest hills cast long, brown shadows across the expanse of blue glass. A breeze gathers momentum. Another cool day is expected.

After extinguishing the fire I locate a small river on a topo map. Local fishermen had sung the praises of a favorite pool several miles north, lost in a small canyon. They were right to do so, I discover the next day. Sculpted through granite by the hand of time, it is idyllic and, at the moment, uninhabited by other anglers.

I wade into the chilling water and tie on a Muddler Minnow. Standing in the elbow of the fast-flowing stream I am lost, once again, in the beauty beyond. There is a bigness about this country—miles of unscathed rivers and streams; pockets of isolated lakes; vast, dense acres of white spruce and fir with spires that rise to the clouds, nearly brushing their bottoms.

Food and shelter grow here for countless forms of wildlife. Low, protective sumac, dense briar, rushes, reeds, berries, trees, and leaves support Canada geese, mallard, heron, loons, songbirds, otter, beaver, fish, moose, bear, mice, and rabbits—all a necessary balance contributing to the ever-changing cycle of life in the wilderness. Almost as punctuation to my thoughts, a bull moose strolls out of a dark thicket for a drink of cool stream water. He is not concerned with my presence; he is intent upon quenching his thirst. Perhaps it was a long trek through the thick sumac.

I remain still and let my line drift unattended. I do not want a fish to hit now and disturb the scene. What a creature. Six or seven feet tall, close to a thousand pounds, and displaying huge, palmate antlers nearly as wide as his body is long, the moose stands on thin, gangly legs that look ill-equipped to bear such a heavy, awkward mass. I fear he may collapse any minute.

He disgorges an underwater rock with his nearly bifid nose, looking for a treat, then raises his head and looks straight at me. From a mere thirty yards away I watch the water gushing down his beard and wonder if he is considering a charge. I reflect briefly on a warning issued in a Henry David Thoreau essay: "Moose are dangerous to encounter and will not turn out . . . but furiously rush upon [man] and trample him to death, unless he is lucky enough to avoid them by dodging around a tree." Hmm. I look around. I look down at the water I am standing in, in these cumbersome waders. No trees here. Think I'll just be still. Real still—I wouldn't want to be the first to initiate aggressive behavior. Slow minutes pass. The moose takes another drink, lifts his head, looks in another direction, stops ruminating, and finally begins to move away from me, unrattled and seemingly in no hurry. His casual attitude leads me to believe he will continue sloshing his way downstream. And spare me.

He moves on, stopping occasionally to disinter some tasty crustacean and popping his head up to look around. Could he, too, be awestruck by this land? Did he decide to follow the scenic trail to the stream this day, or did he choose the well-trodden path because he was thirsty? He slowly disappears around another bend in the river. I think he just wants to continue his journey, peacefully uninterrupted, like me. Thoreau was probably never attacked by a thousand-pound moose.

My fly sways with the motion of the stream, rippled now with moose prints, and I sit, a little numbed, on the river's edge. Once again I have caught no fish, but landed a finer trophy in this everlasting image.

There is a brief, single moment at dusk, after the sun has eased below the horizon, when the sky's hues diminish to pastels and the opposite shoreline fades from blue-green brilliance to no color at all. One instant the horizon line holds color; the next moment the fall hues are steel-black. Eventually, even shadows disappear, bid adieu by the staccato whistle of the loon.

I must leave this woodland sanctuary tomorrow. But I will return to hear the duet of loons penetrating the crisp air of night. Their sound is the song of the north.

Morel, Asparagus & Vidalia Onion Flan

Makes 12 individual flans

THIS SPRING FLAN IS A WELCOME side dish when morels pop up in the woods and asparagus and Vidalia onions first come into the market. If you cannot harvest or buy fresh morels, substitute ¼ ounce of dried mushrooms that have been soaked in water or sherry for about 30 minutes.

Baked flans can be prepared up to 1 day ahead; to reheat, warm in an oven on low (about 300°F.) for about 10-15 minutes, but they really are best served immediately.

3 tablespoons butter

2 small morel mushrooms, finely chopped

4 stems asparagus, about 1 inch of end cut off, finely chopped

¼ cup finely chopped Vidalia onion

1 tablespoon stemmed fresh thyme

½ teaspoon salt

1 tablespoon freshly ground black pepper

2 cups milk

3 large eggs, beaten

Preheat the oven to 350°F.

Heat 2 tablespoons of the butter in a medium skillet over medium-low heat. Combine the morels, asparagus, onion, thyme, salt, and pepper and sauté for 6-8 minutes, until onions are translucent. Remove from the burner and set aside.

In a medium saucepan over medium-high heat, bring the milk to a boil and reduce the flame to medium-low. Slowly add the beaten eggs to the milk, whisking constantly until the mixture is thoroughly blended, about 2-3 minutes. Remove from the burner and stir in the sautéed vegetables.

Melt the remaining 1 tablespoon butter and brush it on the bottom and sides of a nonstick 12-cup muffin tin. Fill the compartments evenly with the flan mixture and bake for about 30-40 minutes or until a toothpick inserted in the center comes out clean.

Remove the muffin tin from the oven and cool for about 10 minutes on a wire rack. Run a pointed knife around the outside of each flan, being careful not to cut into it. Cover a large cutting board with a piece of foil or waxed paper and place it over the muffin tin. Hold firmly in place and turn the tin over onto the board. The flans should release easily. If they do not, you may have to coax them out with repeated tapping. Serve hot.

Flaming Red Pepper & Fiddlehead Flan

Makes 12 individual flans

These flans bake to a colorful pink or light red and make a bright side dish. If you cannot locate fiddleheads, substitute asparagus tips.

1 sweet red bell pepper

2 tablespoons vegetable oil

4 tablespoons unsalted butter

1 small Vidalia onion, finely chopped (about ½ cup)

2 cups milk

3 large eggs, beaten

½ teaspoon salt

1 teaspoon ground white pepper

24-36 fiddlehead ferns, washed and trimmed

Preheat the oven to 350°F.

Brush the red pepper with vegetable oil and hold it over the flame of a gas burner, skewered (or place it on a broiling pan, 2-3-inches under a broiler). Roast it on all sides until blackened. Transfer to a paper or plastic bag, seal, and set aside for about 10 minutes.

Peel the black skin from the pepper and discard. Cut the pepper in half, seed, devein, and finely chop. Melt 2 tablespoons of butter in a small pan and add the chopped onion and the red pepper. Sauté for 6-8 minutes, until onions are translucent. Purée the mixture in a food processor until smooth.

Bring the milk to a boil in a medium saucepan over medium-high heat. Immediately turn down the flame to medium-low. Slowly add the beaten eggs to the milk, whisking constantly until the mixture is thoroughly heated, about 2-3 minutes. Turn off the heat and remove the pan from stove. Mix in the onion-red pepper puree, the salt, and pepper and whisk together.

Melt the remaining 2 tablespoons of butter and brush it on the bottom and sides of all compartments in a 12-cup muffin tin.

Trim the fiddleheads to fit in the muffin tin by cutting off about one-quarter of the stem. Lay 2-3 ferns in the bottom of each compartment, fanned out symmetrically. Fill the compartments with the flan mixture, being careful not to disturb the ferns, and bake for 30-40 minutes, until a toothpick inserted in the center comes out clean.

Remove the tin from the oven and cool for about 10 minutes on a wire rack. Run a pointed knife around the outside of each flan, being careful not to cut into them. Cover a large cutting board with a piece of foil or waxed paper and place it over the muffin tin. Hold firmly in place and turn the tin over onto the board. The flans should release easily. If they do not, you may have to coax them out with repeated tapping. Serve hot.

Desserts

Peach Tart

EVERY SATURDAY IN THE SUMMER during the Tanglewood music festival, Konkapot Restaurant hosted a catered canoe trip. We would meet the dozen or so sporting souls on the shore of the Housatonic River and guide them downstream to a picturesque covered bridge for the picnic; afterward, we sent them off to Tanglewood with a box supper.

These picnics featured relaxing music, a filling picnic, and the following dessert, which became standard fare.

To make the pastry: Combine the flour, sugar, salt, cloves, and zest in a large mixing bowl. Using two butter knives, cut in the butter until the mixture resembles coarse crumbs. Mix in the egg yolk and ⅓ cup of cold water. Mix well, wrap the dough in plastic wrap, and refrigerate for about 1 hour.

Preheat the oven to 400°F.

To make the frangipane: Pulverize the almonds for 1 minute in a food processor or blender. Add the egg whites, sugar, and almond extract. Process for about 30 seconds.

To make the filling, combine the peaches, sugar, and cinnamon in a large bowl. Stir together and set aside.

Roll the pastry out into a 16 x 12-inch oval, carefully slide it onto a baking sheet, and spread the frangipane over the entire surface. Place the fruit neatly in overlapping rows on top. Fold 2 inches of dough all around the edges to create a border and hold in the juices. Dot the fruit with the butter. Bake for 50-60 minutes, until the fruit is soft and the pastry is lightly browned.

Melt the apricot jam, Triple Sec, and ¼ cup of water together in a small saucepan to make a glaze. After removing from the oven, brush or drizzle the warm glaze over the entire surface of the fruit.

FOR THE PASTRY

2 cups flour

1 teaspoon granulated sugar

½ teaspoon salt

½ teaspoon ground cloves

2 teaspoons grated orange zest

½ cup unsalted butter, cut into 8 pieces

1 egg yolk

FOR THE FRANGIPANE

1 cup blanched, slivered almonds

2 egg whites

¾ cup powdered sugar

½ teaspoon pure almond extract

FOR THE FILLING

1¾ pounds peaches, pitted and cut into eighths

2 tablespoons granulated sugar

1 teaspoon ground cinnamon

2 tablespoons unsalted butter, cut into small pieces

FOR THE GLAZE

½ cup apricot jam

1 tablespoon Triple Sec, Cointreau, or orange curaçao

Plum Crisp

Serves 8

8 cups seeded and quartered plums
(about 2½ pounds whole)

¼ cup maple syrup or honey

⅓ cup Triple Sec or other orange-
flavored liqueur

1 teaspoon cinnamon

1 teaspoon freshly grated nutmeg

1½ cups brown sugar

1 cup flour

⅓ cup rolled oats

12 tablespoons (¾ cup) unsalted
butter, cut into ½-inch chunks

MOST PEOPLE SEEM TO LOVE PLUMS, especially when cooked. I often use plums instead of peaches in my Peach Tart recipe (see previous page), and one could easily use peaches in this recipe.

Unlike a tart, a crisp has the "pastry" on top.

*P*reheat the oven to 375°F.

Combine the plums, maple syrup, Triple Sec, cinnamon, and nutmeg in a large bowl. Stir, coating the plums completely, and set aside.

Combine the brown sugar, flour, and oats in another large bowl or the bowl of a food processor equipped with a plastic blade. Mix together thoroughly and add the butter chunks. Either cut in the butter with two butter knives or pulse several times in the food processor until the mixture resembles a coarse meal. Do not overwork.

Pour the fruit and its juices into a 9 x 9 x 2-inch glass or ceramic baking pan and level it. With a spoon or your fingers, spread the brown sugar–flour mixture evenly over the top. Transfer to the oven and bake for about 1 hour, until the top is browned.

Remove the crisp from the oven and let it cool about 20 minutes before serving. Serve with freshly whipped cream.

Apple Cobbler with a Buttermilk Crust

YOU WILL NOTICE THAT WHILE MIXING the cobbler crust, it will seem runny, but that is normal. It bakes to a crumbly biscuit finish. This seemingly common dessert is not only delicious, but fit for a king or queen.

*P*reheat the oven to 400°F

Combine the flour, sugar, baking powder, and salt in the bowl of a mixer equipped with a dough blade. Turn on low, mix for about 30 seconds, then add the butter. Process until the mixture resembles a coarse meal.

In a small bowl mix together the buttermilk, egg, and zest with a fork or wire whisk. Slowly add to the flour mixture and continue mixing until fully incorporated (do not mix longer than necessary or the dough will toughen). Set aside.

Combine the apples, sugar, flour, nutmeg, and zest in a large bowl and gently mix together. Pour into a 9-inch round glass or porcelain tart or pie pan at least 1 ½ inches high. Spread evenly and dot with butter.

With a large spoon, ladle the dough on top of the fruit in several small mounds until the entire pan is covered.

Bake on the middle shelf of the oven for about 40 minutes or until the top is browned. Remove and let cool for at least 15 minutes before serving. Serve with freshly whipped cream, crème anglaise, or ice cream.

FOR THE CRUST

1¼ cups flour

½ cup sugar

1 teaspoon baking powder

½ teaspoon salt

4 tablespoons unsalted butter, chilled and cut into small pieces

½ cup buttermilk

1 large egg

Zest from ½ lemon

FOR THE FILLING

6 small McIntosh apples, peeled, cored, and sliced (about 6 cups)

¼ cup sugar

2 tablespoons flour

1 teaspoon freshly grated nutmeg

Zest from ½ lemon

2 tablespoons unsalted butter, cut into small pieces

Orange Custard

THIS RICH BAKED CUSTARD, flavored with orange, should be baked in a glass or ceramic baking dish. After it has been chilled, it can be sliced like a tart.

2½ cups heavy cream

1 tablespoon orange curaçao or Triple Sec

Zest of 1 orange, finely diced

3 eggs

4 egg yolks

⅓ cup sugar

1 teaspoon vanilla

Fresh mint sprigs, for garnish

Preheat the oven to 325°F.

Heat the cream with the orange liqueur and zest in a heavy saucepan over medium heat until barely simmering, about 5 minutes. Do not boil.

While the cream is heating combine the whole eggs, yolks, sugar, and vanilla in a large bowl. Stir with a fork until thoroughly mixed.

Slowly pour the heated cream into the egg mixture. Stir gently with a fork or spoon. Do not use a wire whisk, which can cause air bubbles to form. Pour the mixture into a 9-inch round ceramic or glass pie plate. Carefully cover with aluminum foil, not letting the foil touch the custard. Set into a larger baking pan containing about ½ inch of water to avoid burning the bottom and sides of the custard.

Bake for 40-50 minutes, or until a knife comes out clean when inserted into the custard toward the edge of the pan. The center will still be slightly soft, but will finish cooking as it cools. Remove from the oven and let rest for about 15 minutes before removing the foil.

When completely cooled, cover with plastic wrap and refrigerate overnight.

Remove the custard from the refrigerator and set aside for few minutes.

Cut custard into 8 slices and place one slice on each plate. (You can warm it slightly in a microwave if you wish, but do so carefully so it doesn't melt.) Garnish each serving with a sprig of fresh mint.

Cooking Notes & Basic Recipes

Gaminess

Big game meat can be difficult to cook. It's hard to decide the cooking time; whether to marinate or not; and how to cook it—to sauté, grill, roast, braise, or stew. Many factors influence whether meat will be tough or tender, tasty or terrible—the condition of the kill, the time of year (before or after the rut, a strong determinant of flavor), and the animal's sex, age, and diet. The hunter himself will have a better sense of the condition of the animal because he knows the circumstances of the kill. Whenever possible, find out these critical facts before planning a wild game dinner.

"Gaminess" is a word that needs clarification. I don't believe people agree on what it is. After many years of introducing customers to new tastes in wild game, I find most people say something is "gamy" because it does not taste like the beef, veal, or lamb they are used to eating—animals that have been farm-raised, for the most part, on grains.

Webster's Dictionary describes "gamy" as "having the flavor of game, especially game that has been kept raw until somewhat tainted . . ." I disagree; it does not have to be tainted. Again, from *Webster's Dictionary*, taint means: "to imbue with an offensive, noxious or deteriorating quality or principle; infect with decay . . ." "Gamy" may mean many things, but mostly it refers to tastes that depend on how an animal lived and was killed, gutted, hung, and aged.

In the best of circumstances, the game you enjoy will have had a good, clean kill (swift, with no delay in the dying process—which agitates the adrenalin level, skilled gutting (without puncturing the intestines or the bladder, possibly contaminating the surrounding meat), careful and clean handling (dirt and hair harbor bacteria that can infect the meat), cool weather (for handling and transporting the carcass without spoilage), cool surroundings while hanging, and finally, once again, cleanliness—controlling bacteria by eliminating as many foreign contaminants as possible when meat is handled.

The diet of the animal also affects flavors. A yearling that has been calmly grazing in fields since birth and is killed early in the season may taste better than an old 10-point buck that barely survived a winter with a 50-inch snow-cover that buried much of his food supply.

The actual flavor of meat, as any cook knows, can be altered by the use of marinades, curing, smoking, adding herbs and spices, and by the actual cooking process. I prefer to experience the inherent flavor of meat or fish first. Then I might try adding sauces, herbs, spices, or marinades.

A hunter once told me how much he hated the taste of caribou—which I find one of the tastiest big game meats. He later told me how many times he had shot at the animal before delivering the killing blow. I'm sure that animal's adrenaline flow caused his dislike.

I hope some of the recipes in this book provide some new and some old techniques of cooking wild game—meats, fowl, and fish.

To Prepare a Backyard Smoker

Suspend a tray containing about 1½-inches of water and a handful of hardwood chips over the fire. Most grill/smokers come equipped with this tray, but if yours does not, use an old aluminum baking pan about 2-inches deep that will fit inside the grill, under the grate.

Fruitwoods—such as apple and cherry—are the best woods for smoking, but any hardwood or dried grapevines will create sweet smoke, not as harsh as mesquite or hickory (which should be reserved for hams, Canadian bacon, ribs, and larger cuts of meat).

To Bone a Whole Cooked Fish

With the fish lying on one side, remove the backbone. Insert a thin, sharp knife along one side of the backbone near the head and cut toward the tail, keeping the blade angled downward and holding it as close to the bone as possible—actually scraping it. Carefully fold back the top fillet onto the cutting surface. This will expose the entire backbone, which can be easily lifted off the bottom fillet. Discard the bone. Remove the larger bones along the belly with your fingers and reassemble the fish to appear whole. To serve, cut into individual pieces across the grain.

To Prepare a Charcoal Grill

Use only unadulterated charcoal, not the kind impregnated with lighter fuel.

Start the fire using paper or small twigs, never charcoal lighter fluid, which imparts an unpleasant petroleum flavor to foods.

To avoid flare-ups from oil, butter or fat dripping into the fire, keep a spray bottle of clean water handy—like the one you use to mist indoor plants. A gentle spray will put out unwanted flames.

Keep the grate of the grill clean, primarily for health reasons. Bits and pieces of food sitting out in warm temperatures can attract flies and harbor bacteria growth. If you brush a little oil on a clean grill before heating, it will make cleaning the grill much easier.

Replace charcoal and wood chips as necessary throughout the grilling and smoking process. Do not grill in an enclosed area.

Corn & Tomatillo Sauce

Tomatillos, a mainstay of Mexican cooking, have a slight bitter-lemon taste. You may want to parboil them for a few minutes before grilling. The corn serves as the binder and also provides a milky sweetness. You can puree the sauce, but I prefer it a little chunky.

You can freeze this sauce or it will keep refrigerated for up to 3 days—longer, if you use stock in place of cream.

2 ears of fresh corn, husked, or 1 cup canned
    corn kernels, drained
8 tomatillos, husk removed
1-2 small jalapeño peppers
1 large ripe tomato
vegetable oil for brushing
1 tablespoon butter
1 medium white onion, finely chopped (about 1 cup)
4 garlic cloves, finely chopped
1 teaspoon salt
1 teaspoon black pepper
½ cup heavy cream, veal, or chicken stock

Light a charcoal fire in an outdoor grill. When the charcoal is gray and hot, place the corn, tomatillos, jalapeños, and the tomato on the grill. Brush the vegetables with oil, cover, and roast for about 15 minutes, turning once and brushing again with the oil. Remove and peel the tomato while still warm. Dice the tomato, peppers, and tomatillos, and set aside.

Strip the kernels from the corn by cutting away from you with a sharp knife over a bowl. Quarter the jalapeño peppers and remove the seeds and veins. (Leave them in if you prefer a hotter sauce).

Melt the butter in a medium saucepan over medium-low heat and sauté the onion and garlic for 6-8 minutes, until translucent. Add the tomato, corn, peppers, tomatillos, salt, and pepper and sauté for another 5 minutes. Add the cream, stir, bring to a boil, and reduce by one-half, about 10 minutes. Ladle over fish or fowl and serve hot.

Serves 6-8.

Toasted Pecan & Corn Gravy

I first used this versatile sauce on catfish, but it's great with venison tenderloin or wild boar chops.

1½ teaspoons vegetable oil
½ cup coarsely chopped pecans
2 tablespoons butter
1 medium onion, finely chopped (about 1 cup)
2 ears fresh corn or 1½ cups corn kernels, drained
2 garlic cloves, finely chopped
¾ cup low-salt veal or beef stock
¼ cup heavy cream
2 tablespoons molasses or maple syrup
1 tablespoon ground cumin
1 teaspoon curry powder
Pinch of cayenne (more if you like it hot)
Salt
1 teaspoon cracked black peppercorns
1 tablespoon garam masala (optional; see Mail-Order Sources)

Heat 1 teaspoon of the vegetable oil in a medium sauté pan over medium-high heat until it begins to smoke. Add the pecans and toast for 3-4 minutes, until lightly browned, watching carefully so they do not burn.

Transfer to paper towels to drain.

Turn the heat down to low and place the butter and ½ teaspoon of oil in the pan over medium-low heat. Add the onions, corn, and garlic. Sauté for 6-8 minutes, until the onions are translucent, then add the stock, cream, and molasses. Raise the heat to medium-high and reduce by one-third, 8-10 minutes.

Add the cumin, curry, cayenne, salt to taste, the pepper, garam masala, and ¼ cup pecans to the pan. Heat for about 1 minute on low. If the sauce is too thick, thin with more veal stock or cream.

Serve by pouring the sauce over meat or fish, and sprinkle the remaining pecans on top.

Serves 4-6.

New Mexican Chile Sauce

THIS SAUCE CAN BE USED with many Mexican dishes. I also add it to pasta sauces (see Smoky Caribou Sauce recipe on page 127).

3 ounces dried New Mexico chiles
1 tablespoon butter
½ small onion, finely chopped (about ½ cup)
4 garlic cloves, finely chopped
1 tablespoon ground cumin
1 teaspoon oregano, preferably Mexican
1 teaspoon salt

Soak the chilies in three cups of warm water for 30-45 minutes.

Remove the chiles and reserve the liquid. Take out all the veins and seeds, which are the source of the heat (if you like your sauces hotter, do not remove all of them).

Melt the butter in a medium sauté pan over medium heat and sauté the onion and garlic for 6-8 minutes, until the onion is translucent. Combine the chiles with the onion and garlic in a food processor and puree for about 30 seconds. Scrape down the sides of the bowl with a rubber spatula, add half of the water from the chiles, and pulse for another 15-20 seconds, until smooth.

Pour the mixture into a large saucepan, add the remaining chile water, and simmer over low heat for about 15 minutes. Add the cumin, oregano, and salt, and simmer for another 5 minutes. Transfer to a container and refrigerate for up to 3 weeks, or freeze in small batches for up to 6 months.

Makes about 1 quart.

Pizza Dough

1½ packages active dry yeast (3¾ teaspoons)
1 teaspoon sugar
2 tablespoons olive oil
1 cup warm water (about 85°F.)
2½ cups unbleached all-purpose flour
¼ cup whole wheat flour
¼ cup yellow cornmeal
1 teaspoon salt
1 handful of: ¼ all-purpose flour and ¾ part yellow cornmeal (for rolling out dough)

In a small bowl, place the yeast, sugar, and olive oil. Add the water, stir, and set aside for 4-5 minutes.

In the bowl of a food processor equipped with a plastic blade, mix together the flours, cornmeal, and salt. Leave machine running and add the yeast mixture, drizzling it in slowly through the feed tube until the contents form a soft dough ball (do not overwork).

Transfer the dough to a large bowl that has been brushed with oil, cover with plastic wrap, and set in a warm place for at least 1 hour, or until double in size. Punch down dough and let rise an additional 45 minutes.

Preheat the oven to 400°F.

Spread the flour-cornmeal mixture on a large cutting board or work area. Roll out the dough, turning to coat with the mixture, until about ⅛-inch thick. Transfer to a pizza pan or peel. Add toppings and bake 20-30 minutes, or until the edges of the dough are crispy brown and the filling is cooked.

Makes enough for two 12-14 inch pizzas.

Curing Solution for Fish

THIS CURE CAN be used with any fish. Cured, smoked fish will keep in the refrigerator for up to 6 days, but it's best when served warm from the smoker.

½ cup dry white wine
¼ cup light brown sugar
12 juniper berries, ground
¼ cup pickling spices
2 teaspoons coarse (kosher) salt
2 tablespoons cracked black peppercorns
Zest of one lemon

Combine 1½ cups water and the wine in a medium saucepan over medium-high heat and bring to a boil. Add the brown sugar and immediately reduce the heat to medium-low. Stir until the sugar is dissolved, about 1 minute. Add the juniper berries, pickling spices, salt, pepper, and zest. Cover, reduce the heat to low, and simmer for about 1 hour. Remove from the stove and strain through 2 layers of cheesecloth into a covered jar. Refrigerate for at least one hour before using.

Makes about 1¾ cups.

Jerk Rub

Many foods are given an extra zip and unusual flavor with this hot (peppers) and sweet (nutmeg and cloves) spice combination from Jamaica. Generously rub into venison or elk chops, swordfish steaks, or pheasant breasts about 1 hour before grilling, baking, or pan-frying.

¼ cup vegetable oil
½ cup Worcestershire sauce
2 tablespoons Tabasco sauce
2 tablespoons dry mustard
3 tablespoons ground allspice
2 tablespoons onion powder
2 tablespoons dried garlic
2 tablespoons cayenne
1 tablespoon ground cumin
1 tablespoon ground coriander
½ teaspoon ground nutmeg
¼ teaspoon ground cloves
1 tablespoon dried thyme
½ teaspoon salt (optional)
1 tablespoon cracked black peppercorns

Combine all ingredients together in the bowl of a food processor. Pulse 4-5 times, scrap down the sides and pulse again 2-3 times. Transfer to a small bowl, cover and set aside so all flavors may integrate for about 1 hour.

Makes ¾ cup.

Acknowledgments

My heartfelt thanks to all who have been patient and helped along the way, especially Starr Ockenga, a professional photographer, author, and gardener. Without her suggestion, I might never have approached Peter Workman to consider the proposal for this book. Peter, along with Leslie Stoker, Artisan's keen-eyed publisher, saw beyond my original idea and encouraged this particular format. My editor, Ann ffolliott, needs to be greatly acknowledged for her skill in compressing too many recipes and stories into too few pages of this book.

Christine Burger's incisive editorial eye, profound suggestions, refreshing spirit, and (always) clever wit became not only helpful but necessary throughout much of this book. And her a cappella rendition of *Goodbye Old Paint*, sung while on horseback in the Rocky Mountains, was a delightful inspiration for the creation of *Whimper*, my one and only poem.

Thanks to Rob Brill, a city editor for the *Albany Times Union* who so generously edited my outdoor writing over the years, steering me straight in many articles, stories, and a short piece of fiction entitled *Photo Finish*.

Jimmy Nejaime's help in bailing me out with some wine suggestions also needs thanks. After tasting more wines than perhaps I should have, I went to Jimmy and asked if he could help supplement my wine recommendations. Jimmy graciously helped me out as I neared my deadline with wines he has tasted and handles in his complete wine shops in Stockbridge and Lenox, Massachusetts, Nejaime's Wine Cellars.

My fishing buddies need recognition because of their often patient understanding that I am not, nor do I proclaim to be, a fishing or hunting maven. I passionately enjoy all aspects of the sports as well as the luxury of being able to be outdoors as much as possible. But I've welcomed the suggestion that I stop my back-cast a little sooner; I've appreciated being shown how to call a turkey; and I'm grateful for the help while trekking across ten miles of rocky mountaintops in Labrador in pursuit of caribou. I believe a sportsman should not feel as if he or she knows all there is to know—hardly anyone does. In a similar spirit, I always enjoyed learning from other cooks we employed in our restaurant kitchens (whether or not we eventually parted ways). The same is true in the out-of-doors—no one can know it all, and I'm often suspicious of anyone who claims to do so.

Thanks to Norman Seymour for checking the facts in my introduction. Norman is a biologist at St. Xavier University in Antigonish, Nova Scotia, and is considered by George Rieger, an outdoor writer-conservationist, to be the most knowledgeable waterfowl biologist in North America.

Lastly I'd like to address Carole Clark's tireless, dynamic spirit. Carole, my former partner, was the driving force behind both of the restaurants we operated together in two states. Even though her spiraling energy wore me out much of the time, most of the (often-times experimental) foods we created, invented, and had fun with might never have seen the light of day without it. Her intensity and forward thinking were the reasons I pushed on some days. Because Carole drove us both, it sometimes seemed, beyond our creative limits, I believe we were successful food people—not necessarily monetarily, believe me, but more importantly, inwardly, from the heart. If it can be said that there is truth in food, Carole Clark excels in honesty.

Carole and I both had trouble writing down recipes, more likely using the time to explore and concoct. I hope readers using this cookbook will see these recipes in a similar light. A recipe can be a springboard. Don't assume any of these recipes are the last word in wild game, or any food. Add a little more cumin if you wish, substitute white wine in place of red, include additional herbs and expand on recipes, but above all, be inventive. Have fun with cooking. What ultimately comes forth can be exciting and should also be enjoyable. Don't worry about too many boundaries. In food, as in art, there are few.

Conversions

Weight equivalents

The metric weights given in this chart are not exact equivalents, but have been rounded up or down slightly to make measuring easier.

Avoirdupois	Metric
¼ oz	7 g
½ oz	15 g
1 oz	30 g
2 oz	60 g
3 oz	90 g
4 oz	115 g
5 oz	150 g
6 oz	175 g
7 oz	200 g
8 oz (½ lb)	225 g
9 oz	250 g
10 oz	300 g
11 oz	325 g
12 oz	350 g
13 oz	375 g
14 oz	400 g
15 oz	425 g
16 oz (1 lb)	450 g
1 lb 2 oz	500 g
1½ lb	750 g
2 lb	900 g
2¼ lb	1 kg
3 lb	1.4 kg
4 lb	1.8 kg
4½ lb	2 kg

Volume equivalents

These are not exact equivalents for the American cups and spoons, but have been rounded up or down slightly to make measuring easier.

American	Metric	Imperial
¼ t	1.25 ml	
½ t	2.5 ml	
1 t	5 ml	
½ T (1½ t)	7.5 ml	
1 T (3 t)	15 ml	
¼ cup (4 T)	60 ml	2 fl oz
⅓ cup (5 T)	75 ml	2½ fl oz
½ cup (8 T)	125 ml	4 fl oz
⅔ cup (10 T)	150 ml	5 fl oz (¼ pint)
¾ cup (12 T)	175 ml	6 fl oz (⅓ pint)
1 cup (16 T)	250 ml	8 fl oz
1¼ cups	300 ml	10 fl oz (½ pint)
1½ cups	350 ml	12 fl oz
1 pint (2 cups)	500 ml	16 fl oz
2½ cups	625 ml	20 fl oz (1 pint)
1 quart (4 cups)	1 litre	1¾ pints

Oven temperature equivalents

Oven	°F.	°C.	Gas Mark
very cool	250–275	130–140	½–1
cool	300	150	2
warm	325	170	3
moderate	350	180	4
moderately hot	375	190	5
	400	200	6
hot	425	220	7
very hot	450	230	8
	475	250	9

Mail-Order Sources

List of Wild Game Purveyors

A. M. Briggs
2130 Queens Chapell Rd. NE
Washington, DC 20018
202/832-2600
Large variety of game

Broken Arrow Ranch
P.O. Box 530
Ingram, TX 78025
800/962-4263
Wild game, free-range products

Boyer Creek Ranch
Barronett, WI 54813
715/469-3394
Venison products: all cuts, jerky, and sausage

Chieftain Wild Rice Co.
Box 290
1210 Basswood Ave.
Spooner, WI 54801
800/262-6368
Wild rice

Classic Country Rabbit
P.O. Box 1412
Hillsboro, OR 97123
800/821-7426
Rabbit

Culver Duck Co.
P.O. Box 910
Middlebury, IN 46450
219/825-9537
Pekin, moulard ducks

Czimer Foods, Inc.
13136 W 159th St
Lockport, IL 60441
708/301-7152
Bear, many varieties of big game

D'Artagnan
399-419 St. Paul Ave
Jersey City, NJ 07306
201/792-0748, 800/DARTAGN
Wild game, smoked game, foie gras, duck and goose products

Dole & Bailey Foodservice
P.O. Box 2405
Woburn, MA 01888
617/935-1234
Large selection of big game

Durham-Night Bird
650 San Mateo Ave.
San Bruno, CA 94066
415/737-5873
Wild game, fowl, wild mushrooms

Foggy Ridge Gamebird Farm
P.O. Box 211
Q13 Highland Rd
Warren, ME 04864
207/273-2357
Quail, chukars, smoked fowl

Game Exchange
107 Quint St.
San Francisco, CA 94124
800/GAME-USA

Game Sales International
P.O. Box 5314
444 Washington
Loveland, CO 80538
800/729-2090
303/667-4090
Large selection of birds and big game

Grayledge Farms
185 Marlborough Rd.
Glanstonbury, CT 06033
800/854-5605
Pheasant, wild game

High Valley Farm, Inc.
14 Alsace Way
Colorado Springs, CO 80906
719/634-2944
Pheasant and quail

Highland Farm
283 Cty. Rt. 6
Germantown, NY 12526
518/537-6397
Venison; also buffalo, quail

John Dewar
753 Beacon St.
Newton, MA 02159
617/442-4292
Variety of big game

L & L Pheasantry
Box 298
Heggins, PA 17938
717/682-9074
Game birds and fresh rabbit

Lukasik Game Farm
Pearl St.
South Hadley, MA 01075
413/534-5697
Pheasant, duck, turkey, smoked game

Macfarlane Pheasant Farm, Inc.
2821 S. U.S. Hwy 51
Janesville, WI 53546
800/345-8348
608/757-7881
Pheasant

Mahmantongo Game Farms
P.O. Box 5
Pillow, PA 17080
717/758-6284
Pheasant and chukars

Maison du Chevreuil
425 St. Paul St. E.
Montreal, Quebec H2y 1H5
CANADA
514/282-1996
Venison

Maison Glass
52 E. 58th St.
New York, NY 10022
800/822-5564
212/755-3316
Mallard, partridge, goose

Manchester Farms
P.O. Box 97
Daizell, SC 29040
800/845-0421
Quail

Maple Leaf Farms
P.O. Box 308
Milford, IN 46542
219/658-4121
Ducks and duck products

Millbrook Venison
Box 133—Veerbank Rd.
Millbrook, NY 12545
800/774-DEER
Venison

Mondo's and Sons
4225 Rainer Ave. S.
Seattle, WA 98118
206/725-5433
Buffalo, boar, game birds; large variety

National Bison Association
4701 Marion St., Suite 301
Denver, CO 80216
303/292-2833
Bison

Oakwood Game Farm
Princeton, MN 55371
800/328-6647
612/389-2031
Game birds, smoked products

Phuel Farms
P.O. Box 154
Sierra Madre, CA 91024
818/255-6856
*Small game birds; big game,
including boar*

Plantation Quail
1940 Highway 15S
Greensboro, SC 30642
800/843-3204

Quattro Farms
Rt. 44
Pleasant Valley, NY 12569
914/635-2018
*Geese, pheasant, muscovy & pekin
ducks, wild turkey, free-range products*

R.C. Western Meats
P.O. Box 4185
Rapid City, SD 57709
605/342-0322
Buffalo

Specialty World Foods
84 Montgomery St.
Albany, NY 12207
800/233-0193
518/436-7603
Game, foie gras, smoked products

Summerfield Farm
S.R. 4, Box 195A
Brightwood, VA 22715
703/948-3100
Game birds

Unique Foods
520 Executive Dr.
Willow Brook, IL 60521
800/789-6474
Large selection of game products

Valley Game and Gourmet
615 W. 100 St. South
Salt Lake City, UT 84104
800/521-2156
Large selection of game products

Venison America
Rte. 2—Box 2660
Elk Mound, WI 54739
715/874-6856
Venison

Wild Game, Inc.
2315 West Huron
Chicago, IL 60612
312/278-1661
Large selection of game products

Wilderness Gourmet
212 S. 4th Ave, Suite 223
Ann Arbor, MI 48104
313/663-6987
Game birds and big game products

Other Sources

Pendery's
1221 Manufacturing St.
Dallas, TX 75207-6505
214/741-1870
Spices, especially Trinidad Masala

Rawson Brook Farm
Montery, MA 01245
508/949-1603
Fresh chèvre

Index

(Page numbers in italic refer to illustrations.)

Accompaniments. *See* Vegetable
  accompaniments
Adirondacks, bear hunting in,
  137–38
Angler, The, 60
Anisette antelope, smoked, with
  orzo, 140
Antelope:
  black bean, wild game, and corn
    chili, 158
  sauce, smoky, 127
  sautéed, with cabbage and
    orange-soy sauce, 141
  sautéed with puffballs and
    pears, 126
  smoked anisette, with orzo, 140
Appetizers, 11–37
  big game heart sautéed with
    chanterelles, 36
  duck, warm smoked, wild rice,
    and oyster salad, 28–29
  duck, wild, terrine with wild
    mushrooms and dried
    apricots, 30–31
  duck confit, 70–71
  escabeche with grilled spring
    onions, 22–23
  fish terrine, bok choy-wrapped,
    18–19, 21
  game pâté, 37
  herring, marinated kippered, 27
  salmon, home-smoked, 16
  smelt, marinated, 17
  see also Soups
Apple:
  cobbler with buttermilk crust, 177
  fish, and corn chowder, 65
  sausage, and onion stuffing, 162
  -smoked wild boar sandwich,
    114–15
  tarte tatin, 172
Apricots, dried, wild duck terrine
  with wild mushrooms and,
  30–31
Artichoke heart puree, 164, 165
Asparagus, morel, and Vidalia
  onion flan, 169
Avocado mayonnaise, 20, 115

Baked:
  bluefish with horseradish
    mayonnaise, 54
  shad with toasted sunflower
    seeds, 56–57
Balsamic, orange, and ginger sauce,
  grilled duck breasts with, 75

Bannock, blueberry, 130
Barbecued mountain sheep ribs, 149
Basque-style pheasant with olives, 90
Bass, 9
  large-mouth, fishing for, 79
  large-mouth, panfried, 50
  striped, fishing for, 46–47
  striped, with snow peas, shiitake
    mushrooms, and rice noodles,
    52, 53
Bean, Leon L., 60
Bean(s):
  black, wild game, and corn chili,
    158
  white, in game cassoulet, 156–57
  white, puree, 163
Bear:
  diet of, 136
  grizzly, 150, 154
  hunting for, 136–39
  pot roast with beer, 134–35
  sauce, smoky, 127
Beef, 9, 10
Beer, bear pot roast with, 134–35
Big game:
  heart sautéed with chanterelles, 36
  see also Furred game; Venison
Bird hunting:
  for duck on Hudson River, 72–74
  for geese in Massachusetts, 78–80
Birds, game, 66–101
  Canada goose, upside-down
    roast, 81
  Canada goose and fiddleheads in
    coconut curry, 77
  diet and flavor of, 8
  dove with dried cherries and
    pears, 95
  game cassoulet, 156–57
  goose, rabbit, and okra gumbo, 145
  grouse, spit-roasted, with wild
    rice, 84
  grouse breast with pecans over
    quinoa, 82–83
  quail, grilled, with mango and
    peach salsa, 98, 99
  quail, grilled, with red pepper
    sauce, 96
  quail sautéed with melon,
    thyme, and red onion, 97
  sausage, apple, and onion stuffing
    for, 162
  turkey, wild, with leeks, savoy
    cabbage, and clementines, 94
  woodcock, grilled, 101
  woodcock sautéed with oyster
    mushrooms, 100
  see also Duck; Pheasant

Black bean, wild game, and corn
  chili, 158
Black Bull, Bob, 9, 128
Blackfoot, 128–29, 151, 154
Blazy, Martin, 24–26
Blueberry bannock, 130
Bluefish, baked, with horseradish
  mayonnaise, 54
Boar:
  apple-smoked, sandwich, 114–15
  chops, grilled, with coconut-lime
    sauce, 123
  roast leg of, 113
Bob Marshall Wilderness (Mont.),
  horseback trek in, 150–55
Bok choy-wrapped fish terrine,
  18–19, 21
Boning whole cooked fish, 180
Booties, 60
Braised pheasant with red cabbage,
  88
Brown, Bob, 117–18, 120
Buffalo:
  London broil, 142, 143
  massacred in nineteenth century,
    119
  natural health benefits of, 9
  pot roast with espresso, 144
Burger, Christine, 150, 151, 153
Buttermilk crust, apple cobbler
  with, 177
B vitamins, 9

Cabbage:
  red, braised pheasant with, 88
  sautéed antelope with orange-
    soy sauce and, 141
  savoy, wild turkey with leeks,
    clementines and, 94
Cabot Trail, 72
Calcium, 9–10
Callaloo soup with cornmeal
  dumplings, 14
Calvados pheasant, 85
Camping, 33–35
  smoking catch and, 35
  stew pot and, 33–34
  wine and, 35
Canada goose:
  and fiddleheads in coconut
    curry, 77
  hunting for, 78–80
  with leeks, savoy cabbage, and
    clementines, 94
  upside-down roast, 81
Cape Breton Island, fishing on, 72

Cape Cod, fishing off coast of,
  46–47
Caramel sauce, warm chèvre in
  puff pastry with, 173
Caribou:
  annual migration of, 119
  big game heart sautéed with
    chanterelles, 36
  black bean, wild game, and corn
    chili, 158
  chops, grilled, with coconut-lime
    sauce, 123
  game pâté, 37
  hunting for, 116–22
  loin, grapevine-smoked stuffed,
    106–7
  pot roast, 104
  roasted vegetable pizza with
    wild mushrooms and, 124, 125
  sauce, smoky, 127
  sautéed with puffballs and pears,
    126
  shepherd's pie, 159
Carrot-ginger puree with orange
  and lime zest, 164, 165
Casseroles:
  game cassoulet, 156–57
  sweet potato, walleye, and onion
    pie, 51
Cassoulet, game, 156–57
Catskill State Park (N.Y.), bear
  hunting in, 138–39
Chanterelles, sautéed big game
  heart with, 36
Charcoal grills, preparing, 180
Cherry(ies), dried:
  dove with pears and, 95
  sauce, grilled wood duck with, 76
Chèvre in puff pastry with caramel
  sauce, warm, 173
Chicken, 10
Chile sauce, New Mexican, 182
Chili, black bean, wild game, and
  corn, 158
Chippewa, 9
Chopin, Frédéric, 46
Chowder, fish, corn, and apple, 65
Chuinard, Donna, 118, 120, 121
Clark, Carole, 28
Clementines, wild turkey with
  leeks, savoy cabbage and, 94
Clothing:
  cold-weather, 78
  of fly-fishers, 58–60
Cobalt, 9
Cobbler, apple, with buttermilk
  crust, 177

Coconut:
  cream, in callaloo soup with cornmeal dumplings, 14
  curry, Canada goose and fiddleheads in, 77
  lime sauce, grilled wild boar chops with, 123
Cod, 9
Compleat Angler (Walton), 60
Confit, duck, 70–71
  game cassoulet, 156–57
Conversion tables, 185
Cooper, Joel, 41
Copper, 9
Cormany, Hal and Charlotte, 116, 121
Corn:
  black bean, and wild game chili, 158
  fish, and apple chowder, 65
  and toasted pecan gravy, 181–82
  and tomatillo sauce, 181
Cornmeal:
  -covered pheasant breasts with tomatillo-tequila sauce, 92–93
  dumplings, 15
  dumplings, callaloo soup with, 14
  "Counting coup," 139
Couscous, smoked hoisin duck legs over, 68
Crisp, plum, 176
Curing solution for fish, 183
Curry, coconut, Canada goose and fiddleheads in, 77
Custard, orange, 178

Danahar, fishing for trout in, 152
Davis, Larry, 118, 121
Debussy, Claude, 47
Deer. *See* Venison
Desserts, 171–78
  apple cobbler with buttermilk crust, 177
  orange custard, 178
  peach tart, 174, 175
  plum crisp, 176
  tarte tatin, 172
  warm chèvre in puff pastry with caramel sauce, 173
Dogs, hunting, 136
Dossier Lake, fishing on, 41–43
Dove with dried cherries and pears, 95
Duck:
  breast of mallard with morels and pistachio-encrusted figs, 69
  breasts, grilled, with orange, ginger, and balsamic sauce, 75
  confit, 70–71
  confit, in game cassoulet, 156–57
  diet and flavor of, 8
  hunting for, 72–74
  legs, smoked hoisin, over couscous, 68
  smoked, wild rice, and oyster salad, warm, 28–29
  wild, terrine with wild mushrooms and dried apricots, 30–31

wild, venison, and elk stew, 160
wood, grilled, with dried cherry sauce, 76
Dudley, Lass, 150, 153, 154
Dumplings, cornmeal, 15
  callaloo soup with, 14

Eel, 9
Elk, 151
  big game heart sautéed with chanterelles, 36
  chops, grilled, with coconut-lime sauce, 123
  chops with fried green tomatoes and macadamia nuts, 132–33
  pot roast, 104
  sautéed with puffballs and pears, 126
  shepherd's pie, 159
  steak in horseradish crust, panfried, 131
  venison, and wild duck stew, 160
Escabeche with grilled spring onions, 22–23
Eskimos, 129
Espresso, buffalo pot roast with, 144

Farm-raised game, 9
Fat, 8
Fiddlehead(s):
  Canada goose and, in coconut curry, 77
  and flaming red pepper flan, 170
Figs, pistachio-encrusted, breast of mallard with morels and, 69
Fish, 38–65
  bluefish, baked, with horseradish mayonnaise, 54
  cooking time for, 54
  corn, and apple chowder, 65
  curing solution for, 183
  escabeche with grilled spring onions, 22–23
  herring, marinated kippered, 27
  large-mouth bass, panfried, 50
  natural health benefits of, 9–10
  pike, grilled northern, with cucumbers and pine nuts, 61
  salmon, home-smoked, 16
  salmon kabobs, potato-wrapped, 48–49
  shad, baked, with toasted sunflower seeds, 56–57
  shad roe, panfried, 55
  smelt, marinated, 17
  stew, 64
  striped bass with snow peas, shiitake mushrooms, and rice noodles, 52, 53
  swordfish, grilled, with blood orange mayonnaise, 62, 63
  terrine, bok choy-wrapped, 18–19, 21
  trout grilled in foil, 44–45
  trout sautéed with morels and spring onions, 40

walleye, sweet potato, and onion pie, 51
  whole cooked, boning, 180
Fishing:
  campsites and, 33–35
  for cutthroat trout in Rocky Mountains, 152
  fly, clothing for, 58–60
  fly, in north woods of Minnesota, 166–68
  for large-mouth bass in Massachusetts, 79
  music and, 46–47
  in Ontario "bush," 41–43
  salt-water, at Puerto Escondito, 24–26
  salt-water, off Cape Cod, 46–47
  stream, 46
Flaming red pepper and fiddlehead flan, 170
Flans:
  flaming red pepper and fiddlehead, 170
  morel, asparagus, and Vidalia onion, 169
Flathead, 151, 154
Fluoride, 9
Fly-fishing:
  clothing for, 58–60
  nature of, 58
  in north woods of Minnesota, 166–68
Forest fires, 41
Franklin, Judith, 150, 152
French Canadian pea soup, 12
French dishes:
  Basque-style pheasant with olives, 90
  tarte tatin, 172
Fruit:
  stewed pheasant with parsnips and, 89
  see also specific fruits
Furred game, 102–60
  adding fat to, 105
  antelope, sautéed, with cabbage and orange-soy sauce, 141
  antelope, smoked anisette, with orzo, 140
  bear pot roast with beer, 134–35
  big game heart sautéed with chanterelles, 36
  black bean, wild game, and corn chili, 158
  boar, apple-smoked, sandwich, 114–15
  boar, roast leg of, 113
  boar chops, grilled, with coconut-lime sauce, 123
  buffalo London broil, 142, 143
  buffalo pot roast with espresso, 144
  caribou, roasted vegetable pizza with wild mushrooms and, 124, 125
  caribou, sautéed, with puffballs and pears, 126
  caribou sauce, smoky, 127

elk chops with fried green tomatoes and macadamia nuts, 132–33
  elk steak in horseradish crust, panfried, 131
  farm-raised, 9
  game cassoulet, 156–57
  game pâté, 37
  gaminess of, 179
  mountain sheep ribs, barbecued, 149
  mountain sheep stew with caramelized onions, 148
  pemmican, Sioux, 111
  rabbit, goose, and okra gumbo, 145
  rabbit sautéed with rosemary, 146–47
  shepherd's pie, 159
  see also Venison

Gaiters, 60
Game:
  diet and flavor of, 8
  farm-raised, 9
  natural health benefits of, 9–10
  see also Birds, game; Furred game; *specific game*
Gaminess, 179
Ginger:
  carrot puree with orange and lime zest, 164, 165
  orange, and balsamic sauce, grilled duck breasts with, 75
Gitksans, 9
Goat. *See* Mountain sheep or goat
Goose:
  Canada, and fiddleheads in coconut curry, 77
  Canada, upside-down roast, 81
  game cassoulet, 156–57
  hunting for, 78–80
  rabbit, and okra gumbo, 145
Gordon, Theodore, 58, 60
Goulash, venison, 112
Grapevine-smoked stuffed venison loin, 106–7
Gravy, toasted pecan and corn, 181–82
Grilled:
  boar chops with coconut-lime sauce, 123
  duck breasts with orange, ginger, and balsamic sauce, 75
  northern pike with cucumbers and pine nuts, 61
  quail with mango and peach salsa, 98, 99
  quail with red pepper sauce, 96
  salmon kabobs, potato-wrapped, 48–49
  swordfish with blood orange mayonnaise, 62, 63
  trout in foil, 44–45
  venison kabobs in satay sauce, 109
  woodcock, 101
  wood duck with dried cherry sauce, 76

Grills, charcoal, 180
Grizzly bear, 150, 154
Grouse:
　　breasts, cornmeal-covered, with
　　　tomatillo-tequila sauce, 92–93
　　breast with pecans over quinoa,
　　　82–83
　　diet and flavor of, 8
　　with dried cherries and pears, 95
　　spit-roasted, with wild rice, 84
　　spit-roasting at campsite, 35
Guinea hen breasts, cornmeal-
　　covered, with tomatillo-
　　tequila sauce, 92–93
Gumbo, rabbit, goose, and okra, 145

Hall, Irene, 118, 120, 121
Hats, of fly-fishers, 58
Hawk Air, 41–42, 43
Heart, big game, sautéed with
　　chanterelles, 36
Hemingway, Ernest, 25
Herring, marinated kippered, 27
Hoisin smoked duck legs over
　　couscous, 68
Home-smoked salmon, 16
Horseback trek, in Rocky
　　Mountains, 150–55
Horseradish:
　　crust, panfried elk steak in, 131
　　mayonnaise, baked bluefish
　　　with, 54
Hudson River, hunting for duck on,
　　72–74
Hunting:
　　in ancient times, 8–9
　　for bear, 136–39
　　camping and, 33–35
　　for caribou in Labrador, 116–22
　　dogs in, 136
　　for duck on Hudson River, 72–74
　　for goose in Massachusetts, 78–80
　　respect for prey in, 122

Insects, 42–43
Iodine, 9
Iron, 9
Irving, Washington, 60

Jerk rub, 183
Jerusalem artichoke soup, 13
Junction Mountain, 152

Kabobs:
　　salmon, potato-wrapped, 48–49
　　venison, grilled, in satay sauce,
　　　109
Konkapot River, fishing in, 46

Labrador, hunting for caribou in,
　　116–22
Lake Superior, camping on shore
　　of, 33–35

Lamb, 10
Leeks:
　　pheasant with pears and, 86, 87
　　wild turkey with savoy cabbage,
　　　clementines and, 94
Lime-coconut sauce, grilled wild
　　boar chops with, 123
Lodgepole Gallery (near Browning,
　　Mont.), 128–29
London broil, buffalo, 142, 143
Loons, 166–67

Macadamia nuts, elk chops with
　　fried green tomatoes and,
　　132–33
MacLean, Norman, 58
McMenaminan, Don, 153, 154
Magnesium, 9
Mail-order sources, 186–87
Main courses:
　　antelope, sautéed, with cabbage
　　　and orange-soy sauce, 141
　　antelope, smoked anisette, with
　　　orzo, 140
　　bear pot roast with beer, 134–35
　　black bean, wild game, and corn
　　　chili, 158
　　bluefish, baked, with horseradish
　　　mayonnaise, 54
　　boar, apple-smoked, sandwich,
　　　114–15
　　boar, roast leg of, 113
　　boar chops, grilled, with
　　　coconut-lime sauce, 123
　　buffalo London broil, 142, 143
　　buffalo pot roast with espresso,
　　　144
　　callaloo soup with cornmeal
　　　dumplings, 14
　　Canada goose, upside-down
　　　roast, 81
　　Canada goose and fiddleheads in
　　　coconut curry, 77
　　caribou, roasted vegetable pizza
　　　with wild mushrooms and,
　　　124, 125
　　caribou, sautéed, with puffballs
　　　and pears, 126
　　caribou sauce, smoky, 127
　　dove with dried cherries and
　　　pears, 95
　　duck breasts, grilled, with
　　　orange, ginger, and balsamic
　　　sauce, 75
　　duck confit, 70–71
　　duck legs, smoked hoisin, over
　　　couscous, 68
　　elk chops with fried green toma-
　　　toes and macadamia nuts,
　　　132–33
　　elk steak in horseradish crust,
　　　panfried, 131
　　fish, corn, and apple chowder, 65
　　fish stew, 64
　　game cassoulet, 156–57
　　grouse, spit-roasted, with wild
　　　rice, 84

grouse breast with pecans over
　　quinoa, 82–83
large-mouth bass, panfried, 50
mallard, breast of, with morels
　　and pistachio-encrusted
　　figs, 69
mountain sheep ribs, barbecued,
　　149
mountain sheep stew with
　　caramelized onions, 148
pea soup, French Canadian, 12
pheasant, braised, with red
　　cabbage, 88
pheasant, Calvados, 85
pheasant, smoked breast of,
　　salad, 91
pheasant, stewed, with parsnips
　　and fruit, 89
pheasant breasts, cornmeal-
　　covered, with tomatillo-
　　tequila sauce, 92–93
pheasant with leeks and pears,
　　86, 87
pheasant with olives, Basque-
　　style, 90
pike, grilled northern, with
　　cucumbers and pine nuts, 61
quail, grilled, with mango and
　　peach salsa, 98, 99
quail, grilled, with red pepper
　　sauce, 96
quail sautéed with melon,
　　thyme, and red onion, 97
rabbit, goose, and okra gumbo,
　　145
rabbit sautéed with rosemary,
　　146–47
salmon, home-smoked, 16
salmon kabobs, potato-
　　wrapped, 48–49
shad, baked, with toasted
　　sunflower seeds, 56–57
shad roe, panfried, 55
shepherd's pie, 159
striped bass with snow peas,
　　shiitake mushrooms, and rice
　　noodles, 52, 53
sweet potato, walleye, and onion
　　pie, 51
swordfish, grilled, with blood
　　orange mayonnaise, 62, 63
trout grilled in foil, 44–45
trout sautéed with morels and
　　spring onions, 40
turkey, wild, with leeks, savoy
　　cabbage, and clementines, 94
venison, elk, and wild duck stew,
　　160
venison goulash, 112
venison kabobs, grilled, in satay
　　sauce, 109
venison loin, grapevine-smoked
　　stuffed, 106–7
venison meat loaf, 105
venison pot roast, 104
venison shanks, 108
woodcock, grilled, 101
woodcock, sautéed, with oyster
　　mushrooms, 100

wood duck, grilled, with dried
　　cherry sauce, 76
Mallard:
　　breast of, with morels and
　　　pistachio-encrusted figs, 69
　　diet and flavor of, 8
　　legs, smoked hoisin, over cous-
　　　cous, 68
Mango and peach salsa, grilled
　　quail with, 98, 99
Margaree River, fishing in, 72
Marinated:
　　kippered herring, 27
　　smelt, 17
Marlin, fishing for, 24–26
Massachusetts:
　　bear hunting in, 136–37
　　goose hunting in, 78–80
Mayonnaise:
　　avocado, 20, 115
　　blood orange, grilled swordfish
　　　with, 62, 63
　　horseradish, baked bluefish
　　　with, 54
Meat loaf, venison, 105
Melon, quail sautéed with thyme,
　　red onion and, 97
Merganser, diet and flavor of, 8
Mexico, salt-water fishing in, 24–26
Mills, Ron, 151, 152, 153
Mills, Schuyler, 154
Mills, Tucker, 151
Minnesota, fly-fishing in north
　　woods of, 166–68
Moose:
　　author's encounter with, 167–68
　　big game heart sautéed with
　　　chanterelles, 36
　　loin, grapevine-smoked stuffed,
　　　106–7
　　pot roast, 104
　　sauce, smoky, 127
　　sautéed with puffballs and pears,
　　　126
　　shepherd's pie, 159
Morel(s):
　　asparagus, and Vidalia onion
　　　flan, 169
　　breast of mallard with pistachio-
　　　encrusted figs and, 69
　　sautéed trout with spring onions
　　　and, 40
Mountain sheep or goat:
　　ribs, barbecued, 149
　　stew with caramelized onions, 148
Muise, Jim, 116, 119, 121–22
Mushrooms:
　　chanterelles, sautéed big game
　　　heart with, 36
　　morel, asparagus, and Vidalia
　　　onion flan, 169
　　morels, breast of mallard
　　　with pistachio-encrusted
　　　figs and, 69
　　morels, sautéed trout with
　　　spring onions and, 40
　　oyster, sautéed woodcock
　　　with, 100

puffballs, sautéed caribou with pears and, 126
shiitake, striped bass with snow peas, rice noodles and, 52, 53
wild, roasted vegetable pizza with caribou and, 124, 125
wild, wild duck terrine with dried apricots and, 30–31
Music, fishing and, 46–47

Napi (Trickster), 129
Natchez, 9
Native Americans, 9, 13, 128–29, 151, 154
"counting coup" by, 139
hunting practices of, 138
Sioux pemmican, 111
Nets, 60
New Mexican chile sauce, 182
New York:
bear hunting in Catskills in, 138–39
duck hunting on Hudson River in, 72–74
Noodles, rice, striped bass with snow peas, shiitake mushrooms and, 52, 53
Norman, Darrell, 128–29
Northern Lights Outfitters, 116–22
Nova Scotia, fishing in, 72

October Mountain State Forest (Mass.), 136–37
Okra:
callaloo soup with cornmeal dumplings, 14
rabbit, and goose gumbo, 145
Olive(s):
Basque-style pheasant with, 90
parsley sauce, 32
Onion(s):
caramelized, mountain sheep stew with, 148
red, quail sautéed with melon, thyme and, 97
sausage, and apple stuffing, 162
spring, grilled, escabeche with, 22–23
spring, sautéed trout with morels and, 40
sweet potato, and walleye pie, 51
Vidalia, morel, and asparagus flan, 169
Ontario:
camping in, 33–35
fishing in "bush" of, 41–43
Orange:
blood, mayonnaise, grilled swordfish with, 62, 63
custard, 178
ginger, and balsamic sauce, grilled duck breasts with, 75
rhubarb sauce, 110
soy sauce, sautéed antelope with, 141
Orvis, Charley, 60

Orzo, smoked anisette antelope with, 140
Oski-Wawa Campground (Ontario), 41
Oven temperature equivalents, 185
Oyster, smoked duck, and wild rice salad, warm, 28–29
Oyster mushrooms, sautéed woodcock with, 100

Panfried:
elk steak in horseradish crust, 131
large-mouth bass, 50
shad roe, 55
Parsley-olive sauce, 32
Parsnip(s):
puree with orange zest, 164, 165
stewed pheasant with fruit and, 89
Pasta, smoky caribou sauce for, 127
Pâté, game, 37
Peach:
and mango salsa, grilled quail with, 98, 99
tart, 174, 175
Pears:
dove with dried cherries and, 95
pheasant with leeks and, 86, 87
sautéed caribou with puffballs and, 126
Pea soup, French Canadian, 12
Pecan(s):
grouse breast with, over quinoa, 82–83
toasted, and corn gravy, 181–82
Pemmican, 9
Sioux, 111
Pepper, red:
flaming, and fiddlehead flan, 170
sauce, 20
sauce, grilled quail with, 96
Perch, 9
Pheasant, 8
Basque-style, with olives, 90
braised, with red cabbage, 88
breasts, cornmeal-covered, with tomatillo-tequila sauce, 92–93
Calvados, 85
game cassoulet, 156–57
with leeks, savoy cabbage, and clementines, 94
with leeks and pears, 86, 87
natural health benefits of, 9
smoked breast of, salad, 91
stewed, with parsnips and fruit, 89
terrine with wild mushrooms and dried apricots, 30–31
Phosphorous, 9
Pies (savory):
shepherd's, 159
sweet potato, walleye, and onion, 51
Pigeons, spit-roasted, with wild rice, 84
Pike, grilled northern, with cucumbers and pine nuts, 61

Pistachio-encrusted figs, breast of mallard with morels and, 69
Pizza:
dough, 182–83
roasted vegetable, with caribou and wild mushrooms, 124, 125
Plum crisp, 176
Pork, 10
Potato-wrapped salmon kabobs, 48–49
Pot roast:
bear, with beer, 134–35
buffalo, with espresso, 144
venison, 104
Protein, 9
Pueblos, 9
Puerto Escondito, Mexico, salt-water fishing at, 24–26
Puffballs, sautéed caribou with pears and, 126
Puff pastry, warm chèvre in, with caramel sauce, 173
Purees:
three vegetable, 164, 165
white bean, 163

Quail:
grilled, with mango and peach salsa, 98, 99
grilled, with red pepper sauce, 96
sautéed with melon, thyme, and red onion, 97
spit-roasted, with wild rice, 84
Quinoa, grouse breast with pecans over, 82–83

Rabbit, 8
goose, and okra gumbo, 145
sautéed with rosemary, 146–47
Red cabbage, braised pheasant with, 88
Reilly, John, 116–22
Rhubarb-orange sauce, 110
Ribs, mountain sheep, barbecued, 149
Rice noodles, striped bass with snow peas, shiitake mushrooms and, 52, 53
Rigby, Jeff, 72–74
River Runs Through It, A, 58
Roast(ed):
buffalo London broil, 142, 143
Canada goose, upside-down, 81
leg of boar, 113
spit-, grouse with wild rice, 84
vegetable pizza with caribou and wild mushrooms, 124, 125
Rocky Mountains, horseback trek in, 150–55
Rosemary, sautéed rabbit with, 146–47

St-Gelais, Julie, 116
Salads:
smoked breast of pheasant, 91

warm smoked duck, wild rice and oyster, 28–29
Salmon, 9
bok choy-wrapped fish terrine, 18–19, 21
home-smoked, 16
kabobs, potato-wrapped, 48–49
smoking at campsite, 35
Salsa, mango and peach, grilled quail with, 98, 99
Salt-water fishing:
off Cape Cod, 46–47
at Puerto Escondito, Mexico, 24–26
Sandwich, apple-smoked wild boar, 114–15
Sardines, 9
Satay sauce, grilled venison kabobs in, 109
Sauces:
caribou, smoky, 127
chile, New Mexican, 182
corn and tomatillo, 181
olive-parsley, 32
red pepper, 20
rhubarb-orange, 110
toasted pecan and corn gravy, 181–82
see also Mayonnaise
Sausage:
apple, and onion stuffing, 162
French Canadian pea soup, 12
venison, in callaloo soup with cornmeal dumplings, 14
Sautéed:
antelope with cabbage and orange-soy sauce, 141
big game heart with chanterelles, 36
caribou with puffballs and pears, 126
quail with melon, thyme, and red onion, 97
rabbit with rosemary, 146-47
trout with morels and spring onions, 40
woodcock with oyster mushrooms, 100
Savoy cabbage, wild turkey with leeks, clementines and, 94
"Scotch double," 80
Scottiglia, 34
Serviceberry soup, 130
Shad, baked, with toasted sunflower seeds, 56-57
Shad roe, panfried, 55
Shaw, Gary, 116-17, 120
Sheep. See Mountain sheep or goat
Shepherd's pie, 159
Shiitake mushrooms, striped bass with snow peas, rice noodles and, 52, 53
Shirts, of fly-fishers, 59-60
Side dishes. See Vegetable accompaniments
Sioux, 9, 129
pemmican, 111
Smelt, marinated, 17

Smoked:
    anisette antelope with orzo, 140
    apple-, wild boar sandwich,
      114-15
    breast of pheasant salad, 91
    grapevine-, stuffed venison loin,
      106-7
    herring, marinated kippered, 27
    hoisin duck legs over
      couscous, 68
    home-, salmon, 16
Smokers, backyard, 180
Smoking, 9
    at campsite, 35
Smoky caribou sauce, 127
Snow peas, striped bass with
    shiitake mushrooms, rice
    noodles and, 52, 53
Sole, 9
Soups:
    callaloo, with cornmeal
      dumplings, 14
    fish, corn, and apple chowder, 65
    Jerusalem artichoke, 13
    pea, French Canadian, 12
    serviceberry, 130
Soy-orange sauce, sautéed antelope
    with, 141
Spit-roasted grouse with wild
    rice, 84
Stainton, Donald, 122
Stewart, Jim, 150, 153-54
Stews:
    black bean, wild game, and
      corn chili, 158
    at camp centers, 33-34
    fish, 64
    mountain sheep, with
      caramelized onions, 148
    pheasant with parsnips and
      fruit, 89
    venison, elk, and wild duck, 160
Stockton, Al, 136
Stream fishing, 46

Striped bass:
    fishing for, 46-47
    with snow peas, shiitake mush-
      rooms, and rice noodles, 52, 53
Strip-mining, 120
Stuffing, sausage, apple, and onion,
    162
Sunflower seeds, toasted, baked
    shad with, 56-57
Sweet potato, walleye, and onion
    pie, 51
Swordfish, grilled, with blood
    orange mayonnaise, 62, 63

Tart, peach, 174, 175
Tarte tatin, 172
Tepee motel, 128-29
Tequila-tomatilla sauce, cornmeal-
    covered pheasant breasts
    with, 92-93
Terrines:
    fish, bok choy-wrapped, 18-19, 21
    wild duck, with wild
      mushrooms and dried
      apricots, 30-31
Thoreau, Henry David, 58, 167, 168
Three vegetable purees, 164, 165
Thyme, quail sautéed with melon,
    red onion and, 97
Tomatillo:
    and corn sauce, 181
    tequila sauce, cornmeal-covered
      pheasant breasts with, 92-93
Tomatoes, fried green, elk chops
    with macadamia nuts and,
    132-33
Trickster, 128-29
Trout:
    cutthroat, fishing for, 152
    fishing for, 43, 46
    grilled in foil, 44-45
    sautéed with morels and spring
      onions, 40

Truro, Mass., fishing off coast of,
    46-47
Tuna, 9
Turkey, 9
    breasts, cornmeal-covered, with
      tomatillo-tequila sauce, 92-93
    wild, with leeks, savoy cabbage,
      and clementines, 94

Upside-down roast Canada
    goose, 81

Valdiviesco, Maurice, 150, 153
Vegetable, roasted, pizza with
    caribou and wild mushrooms,
    124, 125
Vegetable accompaniments, 161-70
    flaming red pepper and fiddle-
      head flan, 170
    morel, asparagus, and Vidalia
      onion flan, 169
    sausage, apple, and onion
      stuffing, 162
    three vegetable purees, 164, 165
    white bean puree, 163
Venison:
    big game heart sautéed with
      chanterelles, 36
    chops, grilled, with coconut-lime
      sauce, 123
    diet and flavor of, 8
    elk, and wild duck stew, 160
    farm-raised, 9
    game cassoulet, 156-57
    game pâté, 37
    goulash, 112
    kabobs, grilled, in satay sauce,
      109
    loin, grapevine-smoked stuffed,
      106-7
    meat loaf, 105
    natural health benefits of, 9

pot roast, 104
sauce, smoky, 127
sausage, apple, and onion stuff-
    ing, 162
sausage, in callaloo soup with
    cornmeal dumplings, 14
sautéed with puffballs and pears,
    126
shanks, 108
shepherd's pie, 159
Vests, of fly-fishers, 58-59
Vitamin B-12, 9
Volume equivalents, 185

Waders, 60
Walleye, sweet potato, and onion
    pie, 51
Walton, Isaac, 60
Weight equivalents, 185
Westphal, Wilhelmina, 111
"Whimper," 155
White bean(s):
    game cassoulet, 156-57
    puree, 163
Wild rice:
    smoked duck, and oyster salad,
      warm, 28-29
    spit-roasted grouse with, 84
Wine:
    chilling, 60
    warming, 35
Winnebago, 129
Woodcock, 8
    with dried cherries and pears, 95
    grilled, 101
    sautéed, with oyster mush-
      rooms, 100
Wood duck, grilled, with dried
    cherry sauce, 76
Woods, Robert "Woody," 117-18, 120

Zinc, 9

DESIGNED BY SUSI OBERHELMAN

Typefaces in this book are
Monotype Dante, designed by Giovanni Mardersteig,
and Twygmond, designed by Joe Treacy

Printed and bound by Grafiche Milani, Milan, Italy